sensitive

The power of feeling
sensitive
in a world that doesn't

Hannah Jane Walker

ASTER*

First published in Great Britain in 2022 by Aster, an imprint of
Octopus Publishing Group Ltd
Carmelite House
50 Victoria Embankment
London EC4Y 0DZ
www.octopusbooks.co.uk

An Hachette UK Company
www.hachette.co.uk

ISBN 978-1-78325-455-2

A CIP catalogue record for this book is available from the
British Library.

Printed and bound in the United Kingdom

10 9 8 7 6 5 4 3 2 1

Senior Commissioning Editor: Natalie Bradley
Senior Editor: Faye Robson
Copyeditor: Caroline Taggart
Art Director: Juliette Norsworthy
Cover artwork: Ian McKinnell
Inside cover image: istock.com/KelvinJay
Typesetting: The Oak Studio
Production Manager: Caroline Alberti

This FSC® label means that materials used for the
product have been responsibly sourced

Printed in Great Britain by Clays Ltd, Elcograf S.p.A.

Contents

For my daughter.
Your sensitivity is your strength.

Scallop Shell by Friða Isberg
(Translated from Icelandic by
my gift daughter Unnur Aldred)

I sensed from the hush
that sensitivity was a weakness
something to hide

so I hid it
not like a sweet
to eat later on

rather like a pale pink
veiny-blue scallop shell
that must not break

Introduction

I guess you're just a little too sensitive. A remark made to me by boyfriends, bosses, friends, taxi drivers, strangers at bus stops – usually smiling, usually kind. Despite the intention, each time it has stopped me short: a slap of shame, a sudden brick wall, a shower running ice-cold mid hair wash. After each encounter, I would think, at what point was it that I showed too much sensitivity? Have I embarrassed myself? Is my face doing something that I don't know about?

It didn't feel like a compliment and I didn't take it as one. Whether people had meant those things kindly or not was irrelevant. I collected these incidents as evidence, and if I had real cause to be sad about something, I would open the box, add some shame to whatever situation I was processing – here is evidence that you are weak, you do not have tough enough skin, you process the world wrong – and conclude, once again, that it was my sensitivity that was the problem.

I didn't do anything with that conclusion, other than self-flagellate and tell my best friend, who experiences the world similarly to me. I found examples of songs and art – other people expressing their own sensitivity, all tortured and in pain – confirming my suspicion that yes, to be sensitive meant to be an eternal outsider, with low self-esteem. The necessity to suppress and conceal this fundamental trait became obvious to me at a young age. I spent my childhood desperate to grow up, bullied at every school I went to.

One day, aged seven, after being beaten up in the bathroom at school, I walked myself out the gates and home to my house. I wrote down in my diary, 'Learn to stop being so sensitive. Until then, pretend you are tough.' When I was growing up, my parents were petrified of how I would find a way in the world. Mum would stay with me at parties, commenting often and ruefully on how difficult I seemed to find just being young, how unsure of myself I was. Later her remarks would change: 'Don't be too hard, Hannah' and 'Remember to be soft sometimes.' I even earned the nickname Knuckles from some friends, hugely ironic and worn with such pride. Faced with society's demands and expectations, and a bloody-minded determination to survive and thrive, I had changed and apparently with successful results. But what might I have lost, and what more might I have achieved, if I hadn't needed to quash my sensitivity in the first place?

In 2015 I had my daughter and something fundamental changed. One afternoon, when I was living in Edinburgh, I stood at the top of a hill in the city's botanical gardens, my sleeping baby strapped to my front, looking out at the hills and spires, and found myself filling up and spilling over with feeling. I was crying because the city's outline was so beautiful, because I was so grateful for my daughter after a long period of infertility and because I missed my family living miles away. I was crying because of the humbling ferocity of parenthood, because I loved my work, my partner, and because becoming a parent meant I could somehow feel again – in fact, it was required of me. It had given me back something I had spent a long time trying to get away from, and it felt like winter sun.

That same day I got an email from a BBC Radio 4 producer called Giles Edwards, asking if I had any ideas for a short piece for a programme. In the fraught time between my daughter napping and waking, I wrote a hurried pitch saying, 'I think sensitivity is an interesting subject. It's shameful.' Giles agreed, and so I started to research. I googled, 'What are sensitive people useful for?' The internet said, 'Intuitive nurturing skills.' In my searches I discovered a popular author and psychologist called Dr Elaine A Aron. She had, after years of research, coined the phrase 'highly sensitive person' or HSP, and concluded that 15–20 per cent of any given population could be labelled as such. There are those who believe it could be as much as 30 per cent. But even if I take the lower end of this statistic, that is one in six. Dr Aron also argued that being 'highly sensitive' is genetic, innate and equally dispersed across all genders and personality types. In other research, I read that the highly sensitive are statistically among a group of people most likely to suffer with mental health problems, to be among our lowest paid employees and not to be politically represented.

While researching and writing the radio text, I would nurse and play with my daughter, take her to playgroups, force myself outside of my social comfort zone for the benefit of her social development. Every game, song and activity presented at these groups, my daughter would sit back and observe. Sometimes, she would remove herself from the circle entirely, and quite literally circle the circle, watching to see what the rules were and if this might be something she would like to do. Sometimes I was embarrassed, and once I stood up, picked her up and rushed out. I wanted her to just join in and, crucially, not show any signs of being at all like me. But she was, and is, just like me. In the Radio 4 piece,

I wrote about the realization that if my daughter was just like me, highly sensitive, and I felt bad about that, then she would learn to feel bad about it too. I was giving her a very hard path to walk. I wrote that I didn't know what to do about it, just that I had to do something. I had to do more, I had to figure out how to have a better relationship with my sensitivity.

The piece aired, and the very day it did emails started appearing in my inbox, hundreds of them. Strangers who had gone online and found my email address on my work website. Extraordinary emails. People asking for and offering resources for other sensitive people, emails sharing page upon page of personal realizations and frustration and life history. There were teachers (a lot of teachers), lawyers, psychologists, psychoanalysts, the head of a world-leading pharmaceutical organization, someone from the UN, someone from the Ministry of Defence, doctors, and a lot of parents worried sick about their sensitive child. I don't really have the words to explain what realizing there were lots of us felt like, contacting them, being taken into their confidence.

After my initial delight, I started to feel very guilty. I hadn't solved anything. I hadn't really changed my relationship to sensitivity. I'd opened a can of worms for a whole load of individuals out there, without offering any real insight, research or progression. I emailed Giles and asked if we could do something more on this, could we make a documentary? It got through all the filter processes at BBC Radio, and we made a full-length radio documentary asking the question, 'How useful is sensitivity to society?' I interviewed a teacher from Hull who, after listening to the initial thought piece, had resigned from her teaching position and taken on another role, realizing that her sensitivity had been thwarting her in her previous job. I interviewed a human resources specialist, asking what she felt the value of sensitivity was to the workplace, and whether the skill of sensitivity should be remunerated on a pay scale if it was proven to be valuable. I interviewed a lobbyist who had created an organization called Vantage, campaigning for equal access rights for highly sensitive people; we talked about whether sensitivity should be considered a disability and have protected status. I interviewed a psychologist researching sensitivity in school and group environments and its implications for bias at work. I interviewed the head of economics at Harvard Business School, who was conducting research into quantifying the value of the skill of sensitivity. I interviewed someone who studies what the brains of HSPs and non-HSPs are doing while processing situations and environments. I interviewed someone who worked in high-end tech system design, and we discussed the value of HSPs to that industry and its development. I answered the question I had set out to ask: 'How useful is sensitivity to society?' The answer was – very.

The programme aired, and I received another batch of amazing emails from strangers. You might have thought at that point I would be content. But no. I knew there was much more to be discovered. We currently live in a society that does not value sensitivity. So undervalued is it, in fact, that many people consider it a guaranteed path to failure, and our attitude towards it becomes self-perpetuating. Nowhere is this more obvious than in employment, where sectors with sensitivity at their heart – teaching, nursing, social work – are badly paid and lacking in social cachet, while in the corporate world the sensitive employee must learn to present themselves in an entirely different way or risk being labelled inadequate.

There are many among us who believe we are living in an epidemic of softness, but the story our society buys into really is that the tough succeed, the winners are rewarded and to win one must be ruthless. We don't know what to do in the workplace when someone makes a decision based on emotion; there isn't a management system for that. We don't know what to do in the classroom when a pupil is sensitive; it slows down teaching. Sensitivity is inconvenient, messy, embarrassing. It is entirely at odds with the professional, technologically centred world we have created. We still promote, above all else, competition, which teaches us to have a fundamental contempt for sensitivity. If anything, we are living in an epidemic of selfishness, not softness. This book considers how we might learn to use sensitivity as a path to forging new selves and a new way of existing – as a strength, a valuable resource, not just in individual self-help contexts, but in the collective social fabric and in the stories we tell about what we value and how we live.

Sensitivity has been written about before, and spaces have graciously and painstakingly been made where sensitive people can feel safe and understood. Exceptional as those safe spaces are, they do not change the narrative that says that sensitivity is useless, weak and has no real-life value. That narrative must change, and it will take more than just the sensitive among us to make that happen.

***

You might think that I have learned as much as is possible about sensitivity, that surely I should be satisfied. But in my journey through this subject I have touched on exciting new areas of research and ideas that stand to change who and what we value. That is why I am writing this, to round out the picture more fully and to share that learning with you.

The personal reason is that I still flinch when someone says, 'I guess you're just a little too sensitive.' As a parent, I feel a fierce need to try and change the conditions that made growing up challenging for me. I want the conditions my daughter grows up in to be better. It is a waste to spend a large part of your life wishing your nature was different, and if I still flinch with shame about my sensitivity, my daughter will flinch at her own nature too. There has to be a better story to be found and I want to find it. Society tells us it is bad to be sensitive. But is it? Is there another way of looking at it?

I realize I am writing the book that I wish had existed when I was a sensitive child, teenager and adult; in a way I am writing to my young self as well as to you. And maybe, or maybe not, it is useful for you to know that I spend a few of my days a walking, talking nerve-ending, a flinching piece of flesh, full of insecurity all ringed around sensitivity. Some days I find it helpful to draw on the thoughts and convictions of those I love and who love me.

One spring morning while writing this book, on a day when the moon was still in the sky and daffodils were growing at the feet of streetlights, I called my closest friend, Dr Emma Short, and I told her that I was too sensitive to write this book, that I could not solve sensitivity, that I was not qualified to be doing this. She said something like the following: 'Look, you moose, you are not writing a book to tell people how to get rid of their sensitivity. You do not need to have fixed it. It does not need to be fixed. You are not suggesting it can be cured or that it should be. You are writing a book that offers some evidence that sensitivity is part of us, that it is useful, that it is a good thing, possibly. You have got to try and ignore the doubt. You are qualified to write this book because you have a lifetime of experience of being sensitive. The book is for people like us, and for people who love them, and for people who are not as sensitive too. You have met all these amazing people who have done this amazing research; just do the homework for us on the subject, tell us what they know, help us piece it together.'

And so, armed with all the love and practicality imbued in that, I am really glad you are here. Let's get going.

Part 1
The Story of Sensitivity

1. Self-worth

I want to help change the story of sensitivity: that is why I am writing this book and I hope it is what has brought you here too. To change a story, you need to understand it and know where it comes from. So where does the idea that sensitivity is bad come from? What are its roots?

I think it's important to begin with what we understand by sensitivity. Robin Skeates, in his paper 'Making Sense of World Art: An Archaeological Perspective', starts by defining 'sense', the first part of the word sensitivity, as 'bodily sensation, apprehended through the sense organs'; and, on the other hand, as mental insight, as in 'making sense'. Seems simple enough, right? But we have made the word sensitive quite complicated. We have loaded it with negative associations. We use it as a veiled and not-so-veiled insult: 'I think you are being too sensitive' really means, 'You are bothering me with your feelings.'

Once someone accuses you of being too sensitive, it is likely you will start thinking of it as a personal fault. A commonly used term is 'snowflake', often directed at millennials. There are more archaic insults in our language, such as wuss, milksop, cry baby – I am sure that you can pepper that list with your own. Societal mores have hooked a load of baggage onto sensitivity.

It's like an overloaded camel given no water and told to make it across the desert – the odds are not stacked in its favour. When we say someone is sensitive or being sensitive, we often mean we do not think they have what it takes to complete a task, that their emotions get in the way of achieving. But to reference back to Skeates's definition, sensitivity is quite simple, unencumbered by value – bodily sensation and mental insight. Seems simple enough, and yet it really isn't. We do not treat the trait as something simple, we treat it as something weak. Something is wrong in the maths of its story. The story of sensitivity within our current culture is one of shame: sensitivity dresses in shame, eats shame, sleeps in a bed of shame. And I am just not sure why it is that way. If that is right. And who that negative association is useful to. There has got to be a better way of framing it, right?

Of the hundreds of strangers who got in touch with me after my radio piece about sensitivity, most wanted to tell me that they had been told by their parents or carers that their sensitivity was a problem, that it equated to weakness and was something that needed to be educated out of them. Often we are formed by the stories we grow up around, as well as what is considered socially acceptable for our variables – gender, ethnicity, sexuality, ableism. I am driven in this book by my own experience. I am a white straight woman living in the West. And there will be people with different variables and cultures who will have different, possibly more challenging, stories to tell.

From the moment we are born, we encounter information that informs our idea about who we are and the world that we live in. By the time a child is about eight years old, they have a template idea of their own traits and personality, and whether they feel like a valuable person – they have developed some idea of individual value. Parents and caregivers significantly influence a child's self-worth; idea of self then informs the child's academic and social behaviour. Children learn the world through information they are given, which they relate to themselves, forming ideas such as 'I am brave/sensitive/funny'. We gather that information from birth, and as we grow, we collect autobiographical information and arrive as our jumbled adult selves with a story about our own skills and nature. We use those stories to make sense of ourselves, our daily lives and our place in the world.

I come from a big family of sensitive people whose defining trait is their sensitivity. My mum is our matriarch; with my dad she has raised four sensitive children and six sensitive grandchildren. My mum had a hard time growing up sensitive, and though she and I talk often and in depth, we have not ever particularly discussed her sensitivity. As the writer of this book, it felt important for me to begin this journey of discovery by trying to understand my own sensitivity and, in order to do that, I need to understand my mum's sensitivity too.

Hannah: Mum, would you please introduce yourself?

Kate: My name is Kate. I am an artist of sorts, I am sixty-seven, I have raised four children and I have six grandchildren.

Hannah: How would you describe your relationship to sensitivity?

Kate: I was born sensitive. As a child in nursery, I was told to stop being such a worry mutton all the time. I have three brothers, all of them wonderfully sensitive. As children, they seemed to sail through life, but I fretted. My mother was very busy with the four of us. She was kind, artistic and had high hopes for us all. I'm not sure she fully understood my needs. Emotion wasn't as openly discussed at that time, in the late 1950s, early '60s.

As I got older, it got worse. Or maybe it was just that I noticed it more. I'm sensitive and always have been – sensitive to what people have said, sensitive in the playground, sensitive to anything my mother said to me. And then I was sent away to boarding school, which crucified me, because being sensitive and reacting in a sensitive way to everything that went on, you had to deal with it on your own. There was no space for you to be sensitive, no one to turn to. Pathetic, really. There were things that saved me at school, like art and athletics and music. But the sensitivity, I cannot stress this enough, it was unbelievably debilitating. It was like a brick wall in front of me all the time that I had to somehow find my way around.

Then I left school and I found I had terrible times in situations that other people seem to manage so well. When I was seventeen my parents moved from Cambridge to Bristol and I refused to go, so I rented a room and worked in an office. I didn't contact my family, as I was so angry with them for moving. I got more and more sensitive; I couldn't find friendships who were supportive. And then I went to art college, which was...such an exposure to your own sensitivity because you're creating, which means exposing your very being to criticism. I found it difficult. And so life went on like that, and situations that other people found so easy, I was in a real pickle about.

On a personal level, throughout my life, I have thrived when I had something big and creative to do and a target, and I could gladly work myself to the absolute bone and be so proud of what I'd done, and then I'd fall into this big oversensitive heap and everything everyone said was like being slapped.

And then more worry, worry, worry – worry about everything. Then I met your father and I married him. I felt huge reassurance from his overconfident, larger-than-life presence, which I later discovered was a ruse to mask just how sensitive he is. He had completely the opposite attitude to life. I found such solace in having you children. But as you each grew, I found I was sensitive to how other people were bringing up their children and I began to worry whether I'd done it right.

Hannah: You did, Mum, you and Dad both did.

Kate: When I had you, of course your birth was very traumatic, while you were being born they said you were in real trouble, but you survived. A bad start – your shoulder was nerve-damaged and you were in a lot of pain for the first year of your life, and you were fretful about everything. And I was very sensitive to what you needed. You were born sensitive too. And as you grew up, we realized you were very sensitive to every situation and social interaction. You were like me in the playground, in the classroom, going to parties on your own, worried, watching. You were bullied at each school. When you were about seven, someone I knew was working at the school as a volunteer and she told me that after you hung up your coat you were literally sliding along the corridor with your back to the wall, I think to avoid being seen. The school couldn't or didn't understand sensitivity and there was no support at all. So we found a way to send you to another sort of school, where you flourished, still sensitive but gaining confidence in certain other areas. As time went on, you remained sensitive but settled more. And being a sensitive person myself, I totally understood the difficulties you were facing, and I worried so much that you would end up like me.

Hannah: Mum, I am like you, and I am happy to be like you.

Mum, when we were growing up, there was this thing that you used to say often: 'It's like being a sponge. And I can't take in any more.' Can you tell me a little bit about what you mean by that?

Kate: Being sensitive I think means that you profoundly absorb other people's worries and sensitivity towards things. I have spent a lot of my life absorbing every single worry or problem of those around me. And if you're not careful, you reach a point where you cannot take any more in, overwhelmed. So, you must wring it out, you absolutely have to have ways to wring the sponge out.

And now I am older, and my children have their own lives and children and problems and joys, my sensitivity, and my empathy towards them, coupled with some significant physical illnesses, has at points been so extreme that I've become quite ill. And it really came to light when I was having counselling that everything I was saying gestured at how sensitive I am, and I slowly started to understand something very central about myself.

Hannah: Where do you think your sensitivity came from?

Kate: My father was a very noble, deep-thinking man, very non-judgemental, would make time for everyone – he could see his grandchildren's characters very clearly, he took time for them, he knew and sensed who needed stories or time away from the rest of the family. My father was extremely kind to me about my sensitivity as a child. My mum was busy with the others, my brothers. I think my sensitivity annoyed her.

Hannah: Did your mum come from a family that did not value sensitivity? Or do you think she was very sensitive but educated out of it?

Kate: I gather her father was a domineering character. There was music, art, creativity in their home, but I don't think discussions about emotions back then, there wasn't room for that sort of thing – it was 'chin up'.

Hannah: I am interested in the parenting of sensitive children. When we were little, you used to send us out the door with a particular phrase...

Kate: Yes, I would say, 'Be kind, be sensitive, look out for others.'

Hannah: I remember talking to Rachel [my sister] and she said, 'Mum says, "Be kind, be sensitive, look after others" and today I held the door at school open for someone in the other year, and they pushed it back the other way on purpose and it hit me full in the face.'

I think we had a home where we were all quite kind to each other and sensitive and looked after each other, but then when we got out into the world, we were a bit confused when people were not living by that same set of principles. If you were to raise us again, would you keep using that phrase?

Kate: No, I am afraid I wouldn't. I'd say to all four of you, 'Look, there are going to be times you will need to push to the front of the queue, take up space, be louder if needed.' There are two times in my life I can remember, both running races, both different outcomes with different techniques. The first, I was ten, an interschool competition, and we were in the race, I was running and I was really near the front and the girl behind me let out a yell, she had tripped over and fallen, and I stopped and went back to help her. Then another time, another race, I was about thirteen, and the whistle went and the girl who was the best runner slipped on the chalk line. And I thought, no, I am not going to stop, and so I ran like the wind, and I won. I won!

Hannah: Do you think that your parents taught you good coping strategies for being sensitive?

Kate: No, but I think they did not understand. Boarding school was not a good environment for a sensitive child – constantly in the company of others, very little time alone, very little pastoral care. Very conscious of the impact your body and movements have on those around you and the interpersonal dynamics of the other children there.

Hannah: How do you manage your sensitivity now, Mum? You have had periods of being ill, but you are quite well now.

Kate: I have learned techniques to manage. I don't do yoga or running but I have learned to try to remove myself from things that will make me anxious, I have learned tactics, more awareness. I reorganize the house, I charity shop, I style things,

I take care of my children and my husband of forty-three years and myself and my grandchildren. I try hard not to put myself in positions where the sensitivity is overwhelming. And I have begun to feel a bit more confident of myself. I've had help – medication has enabled me to get on with life.

Hannah: How do you feel about your sensitivity now?

Kate: It's who I am. It's who I've always been. I am a caring person and can sense other people's needs. I'm always looking for ways to help other people; I feel sensitive to their needs in a way that other people don't seem to always notice. And very slowly I have found a way to get my mind around the fact that if you are sensitive, it is part of what makes you you. It's not something that's happened to you. It's something innate in your character, it's your being. So, you work with it. And you're proud of it.

As my life has developed, I have begun to think, well, maybe I am a little different, let the other types of people get on with it. I'm happy to be sensitive and be in care roles; I am delighted to always have a kitchen table full of people who can talk about their experiences of being a person.

Hannah: Have you noticed in your children and in yourself a tendency to take things to heart?

Kate: Oh, gosh, yes. All of them, and myself too. Whereas seemingly, with other people, a comment was made and they could laugh it off, you guys seemed not to have that skin. I think you were all missing a layer of protective skin. You were all so wounded by others. It was painful to watch sometimes.

Hannah: That must have been hard, Mum. As a parent now, I think I know that feeling of wanting to offer your child all you can for them to be able to navigate the world, and a thick skin is a great advantage. Sending a child out with a metaphorical skin layer missing must have felt challenging.

Kate: Yes, but you all found your way, with lots of wrong turns, and you all care for other people and live your lives very deeply.

Hannah: Do you think being sensitive has any benefits?

Kate: I think that sensitivity has the potential to make people highly creative. For example, although I wasn't a very good designer, there are aspects of styling things that I am much better at than a lot of other people.

Hannah: You make the most extraordinary places, Mum.

Kate: All my sensitive siblings are highfliers in the arts – very highfliers – and I think their sensitivity and mine and all my children's, it's like a capacity for great empathy and connecting and finding meaning. I think it's a gift, a gift that comes with challenges. Such intuition, the ability to analyse deeply, to notice, to see, and often to protect other people.

I think I read situations intuitively. I can often see what's about to happen. Throughout my life, I have often said I don't know how I know this is going to happen, but it is. Often that information has been dismissed, but it always happens. Not like once or twice, I mean so, so often. I think maybe I am reading situations differently. I look for the undertones rather than the overt. I can read the detail of people, the things

22

they might not intend to tell you about themselves, through their body language, their micro-expressions, things they are wearing.

Hannah: Like a detective! Throughout my life, when I have brought friends or boyfriends home, sometimes you have said, 'Watch out for that one', and I have said, 'No, they are great.' And then, always, what you have said comes to pass – always.

Kate: It's the inner witch, Hannah. No, it's just paying attention to how people present themselves to you and really noticing.

Hannah: So, Mum, your parents were sensitive, you are very sensitive, as are your siblings, your children and your grandchildren. That is four generations in a line. What kind of story do you think you have passed on to us about sensitivity?

Kate: I hope I have passed on that it's OK to be sensitive. I'm guessing that I must have or maybe you would not be writing this book.

Hannah: Last question in a minute, Mum, and I just wanted to say, I have never really heard you say much about your sensitivity before – I mean, I knew, but we had not really talked about it. I want to tell you that I think you did an amazing and important thing. Generational narratives can be very strong and run on and on. And I think that what you did, having been given a not-so-great story about your sensitivity, you gave us a good one about ours. You changed the story. I mean, we still found it hard, but you supported us. Thank you.

[She nodded]

Hannah: So, having done a lot of parenting and grandparenting of very sensitive children, do you feel you have any advice to offer any other parents of highly sensitive children?

Kate: I think it's like stroking feathers that have been pushed in all the wrong directions. Like detangling your child's hair when it's knotted in the morning. Soothe them and try and build their confidence, notice the detail of who they are, that is where their strengths will grow from. They are not often like other people, they grow in different ways.

Hannah: Anything you would like to be asked that I have not asked, Mum?

Kate: On reflection, because of the work that you are doing on this book, it's made me think very hard about my own character and how sensitivity has affected my life. I've often thought about what life would have been if I hadn't been so sensitive – and I really wouldn't change it.

Why am I sharing this conversation? On a very basic level, because I am so proud to be made of the same stuff as my mum. Despite how difficult it has been for her to live her life as a very sensitive person, she would not change it. Not only is she an extraordinary individual, but also the type of person she is and the skills she has are phenomenal. She makes homes that people walk into and want to cry because they feel so relieved to be in a place of care and beauty. Not ostentatious, but places made out of non-expensive, carefully chosen materials, places that think about how they make other people feel. My mum may have stopped practising as an artist, but she makes art in everything she does. She knows when people are upset, she can see right through to the middle of a person, what they are saying, what they are not, what they hope, what they fear. She can think through any information, consider all options, understand it from all angles and help a person figure out which way they need to go. She is a wonderful mother, grandmother, friend. She is a knower, one of life's great perceivers, holders, makers. She notices things other people miss.

But I am also telling you this story because I believe things might have been quite different for my mum if she had been given an understanding of her sensitivity, her difference, earlier in life. I think it's profoundly unhelpful to move through the world not understanding why you are experiencing things one way and seemingly everyone else is experiencing them with greater ease. I think it's important that as many of us as possible know about this difference. It can make a huge contribution to the wellbeing of a sensitive individual.

I think that can also help us change any unintentional bad story of sensitivity that we live in. I believe my mum was given a bad story entirely unintentionally; my grandparents were really great people. I think the trait was misunderstood, possibly due to cultural attitudes of the times. Yes, my mum is unusual by virtue of being an individual, but her skillset, her value is not unusual in sensitive people.

It is not unusual for sensitive people to spend a large proportion of their days struggling against life, wishing they were different, wishing that they fitted. I am sure there are sensitive people for whom their sensitivity is not a problem; however, struggling is more common than not. Many sensitive people go through life feeling as though there is a continual brick wall in front of them, and the society they live in, and sometimes the care environments they come from, tell them that they need to just stop being so sensitive. But that is not possible. If you are very sensitive, your sensitivity is the main way you experience every aspect of the world every day. So, when you are told, 'Stop being like that', what you hear is, 'I am wrong, I need to stop being like me, everyone else is managing fine, I need to be like them.' That often leaves sensitive people with poor self-worth. The bigger societal stories that we all live in – such as, the strongest succeed; competition and accumulation of wealth are the priorities – tell that sensitive individual, 'See, there is this whole system and you are just an individual, so the fact you do not fit is your problem and your problem solely.'

I heard my mum say that if she had her time parenting again, she would teach us to be ruthless little bastards, and I really understand that impulse, but I don't agree. I think my parents were right to create a home environment where the individual natures of their children had space and validation, and I realize how extraordinarily lucky I am to have had that. My family home was made up of a big, clattering, chatty table of open-hearted people who would drop in to talk, to be by each other. I had better conditions than my mum did. And I would have had an even better self-story if my mum had had a better story about herself. My parents made sure we received non-judgemental love and care, but I grew up aware of the struggle my mum was experiencing and its impact upon her wellbeing, as well as the story she told herself, that her difficulty was due to her sensitivity. Often our children look for themselves in us, for better or worse. The stories we tell ourselves sometimes become the stories our children tell themselves.

When I get dressed in the morning in front of the mirror,

my young daughter comes and puts her school uniform on next to me. I look at my body: it's very far from what our culture considers to be ideal. It is incredibly tempting to say something negative about it out loud, because I look at myself and feel shame, thinking I should try harder to fit what the culture demands. It is an almost physical effort to keep my lips closed and not to criticize myself. I smile kindly at myself. My daughter looks in the mirror at us side by side, grins and says, 'Our smiles are sort of the same and we both like drawing trees.' And it is like someone has reached in and gripped my heart until the blood stops. I think, she sees parts of herself reflected in me. Physically, emotionally. As I stand here and look in this mirror all I think is, 'Please don't be like me, I wish a much smoother, easier path for you.' And then I catch myself. I heard my mum say quite a lot of negative stuff about herself growing up. She never criticized us for our sensitivity, but she did criticize herself. And I realize that my mum and I are like paper dolls connected at the hands, and that my daughter is too. And that between us we pass down stories about the world, about ourselves. If I don't have a good story about my own nature, my child will learn that, through things she hears or my behaviour, and that will colour how she feels about herself and her own nature. At this moment in time, the very best thing I can do for my daughter, and for my mum, is to get a better story about my own sensitivity. I want to look in the mirror and smile at myself because I understand that my traits have value, and I want my daughter to be able to do the same.

Sensitive people do not exist in a vacuum, none of us do. We live in the society we have created, we live among a matrix of humans. Sure, every single sensitive person has the responsibility to find ways to manage themselves and their existence in the world. It is no one else's responsibility. But sensitive people live lives that are interconnected with other types of people by virtue of just being in the world – they are, like all of us, shaped by the stories they are told about themselves at home, at school, by the values of the society we live in. It is tempting to look at the challenges of sensitive people and say, well, that is their problem if they are struggling, because the world is built this way. And that is what I want to excavate under. Is the world really built this way? Who says so? Why? Is it going to stay that way? I strongly believe that through being human we are all deeply interconnected. That how we treat any trait among us has bigger implications for all of us: it is not just the concern and challenge of the very sensitive. This is about where sensitivity sits in society. It is the impact and influence we all have on each other, what we collectively make and the stories that we tell that keep the world turning round. The stories that grow down generational lines, like strings of DNA.

Explaining and researching sensitivity is an incredibly valuable pastime, and I will touch on some of that, but there are people much more qualified than me doing that research. What I can offer you is my experience of being a very sensitive person and being able to look one way in my family line to a very sensitive mother and the other way to a very sensitive daughter. Together with my siblings and their children, we take great comfort in the mass of us, a little clump of sensitive humans. However, I know there will be a moment in time when I have to say goodbye to my wonderful mum and I am damned if I will wait until the last minute to let her know how wonderful she is specifically, but also how wonderful others like her are. I also know there will be a moment in time when my child will have to face the future without me, and I hope to send her on with a story that will sustain her. I am a storyteller by trade and construction, so what I can do is research underneath sensitivity, excavate it and hopefully pull a better story out.

I think it's important that we understand, value, accept and reframe sensitivity. And so, as for where to step next, I look to understand some of the research work that has been done on this subject. What has already been understood? Where is the research headed next?

2. Highly sensitive

So, what does it mean to be very sensitive? Is it a condition? A skill? Are there just some of us who live life feeling like we are missing a layer of skin? Or is that how everyone is experiencing the world? What do we *know*? Turns out, since the 1970s there has been a massive boom in research on the subject of sensitivity. Most notably and foremost from the brilliant Dr Elaine A Aron, psychologist and author. Aron coined the phrase highly sensitive person or HSP, publishing *The Highly Sensitive Person* in 1996 and going on to write a number of other books and conducting extensive research with Arthur Aron and other colleagues.

The Highly Sensitive Person put sensitivity on the map. It contains extensive research and thinking about sensitivity and concludes that this trait is found in higher concentrations among a proportion of the population, to the extent that it is their dominant defining trait. Aron synthesizes the four characteristics HSPs have in common into the acronym DOES, standing for:

D – Depth of Processing
O – Overstimulation
E – Emotional Intensity, Responsiveness and Empathy
S – Sensitive to Subtleties

Aron's book and website offer a free self-assessment test to assist in determining if you are highly sensitive. It can be viewed at: https://hsperson.com/test/highly-sensitive-test/

The test asks if you agree with statements such as:

- I startle easily
- I find myself needing to withdraw during busy days
- Other people's moods strongly affect me

The Highly Sensitive Person explains that sensitivity is not a disorder, it is a trait. That it is found in equal measure among genders, and in introverts and extroverts alike, but is slightly more likely to be found in introverts. Aron's research suggests it is a genetic trait, and that it can be found across multiple species, including humans. She has shown that one in five people have this trait. It took a while for that figure to sink in – one in five. That is 1.5348 billion people in the world. That's a lot of people. That is not a few people. And since there are so many people with this dominant trait, one of them might be you, reading this book now. And if it is not you, then statistically it is someone or multiple someones in your life – your child, partner, colleague, sibling, friend, parent, the stranger sitting next to you on the bus.

Ironically, though, that vast number are still in a minority in terms of how they experience the world. They are still in the main told that they need to change, that the way they are experiencing the world is wrong. HSPs are quite likely to have spent some of their life feeling different in some way to the majority. They may have noticed that others seem to be experiencing or responding to the world in a way that they do not naturally. And it is inevitable that they may have some feelings of concern about that. Research has shown that HSPs are very likely to struggle with compromised mental health. I am really interested in the extraordinary offer that Aron's books have provided for HSPs everywhere. The ability to name and understand one's own nature – to possibly begin to accept it – is really quite something.

When I first read about HSPs and took the test, I found it at once amusing, sobering and touching. Things I had known about myself but not understood started to make sense, were given a name outside of my own half-formed understandings: 'I can't drink coffee, I go jumpy'; 'I can't watch horror films, I don't sleep for days after'; 'I take things people say to heart'; 'The office manager was about to cry. How did you know? I just know'; 'I get exhausted after being with people for periods of time.' All these things, post learning about HSPs, made sense in a different, cohesive way. It made me kinder to myself, it helped me make better choices. Dr Elaine A Aron made that possible.

In 2019, I was an Associate Artist at the National Centre for Writing. This included a residency at their medieval cottage to work on a project, a piece of theatre about sensitivity. The National Centre for Writing organized a literary salon, and at it I read some poems, talked about what I was there to make, and had some discussion with the audience. After the on-stage portion of the event finished, there was a wine reception. Standing in a group talking at events is a bit of an awkward trial for me, no matter how wonderful the hosts and attendees, and I always feel the two-way pull of those occasions. I simultaneously want to meet new people and to make those people happy and comfortable, and I want to go and be alone, to replenish myself.

In this discussion, on this evening, standing on the edge of the group and hopping from foot to foot was a slight, bearded man. I could see he wanted to talk and was trying to figure out the natural gap in conversation. So, I made an excuse and stepped off to the side to talk to him. He told me he was a writer and that he had recently learned he was highly sensitive. He told me how knowing and understanding his sensitivity had changed his life. He finished by saying, 'Knowing I was not the only one was like the sun suddenly coming in through a dark window and lighting up the whole room.'

His description went right to my heart. I walked back to the cottage that evening thinking what an amazing thing it is that Aron has named and made space for an understanding that can give a man back the sun.

Back in the cottage alone, I started to think about the fact that that man had spent so long without the sun. What the reasons for that might be, how problematic that is. It was late. I got ready for bed, read a while and tried to sleep. At 2am I was still awake, and so I wandered around the cottage, room to room with a tea, settling finally at a desk looking out at the herb garden in the dark. Why was I awake? What was bothering me? I sat and let my thoughts get clearer. A memory snapped in – a conversation I had had with a woman who had contacted me a few years earlier, Philippa Smethurst. Philippa is a psychotherapist specializing in trauma. She got in touch after a short thought piece I wrote about sensitivity aired on the radio. We spoke on Skype because I wanted to know about her work with highly sensitive people, and she told me a story.

'When a highly sensitive person comes into my office, there can be a knot, and part of this knot is the person's shame. There is a lot of shame. Shame constitutes the evidence or messages that the person has received, where the world has told them they are the wrong shape. What I do with them is help them untangle those ropes,' she said.

'What do you mean by ropes?' I asked.

'Imagine ship ropes – big, weighty, functional ropes. They usually have two knotted together, into a big messy ball, seemingly impossible to undo. What I do with them, what we do together, is help them unknot those ropes. One of those ropes is who they are, their traits, their character. And the other is how the world feels about their character traits. The knots are their inner responses to these shame messages. I help them to understand that it is not who they are that is inherently shameful, but how the world feels about their dominant character trait – sensitivity. We untie the knots through understanding, so that the person can leave the session with some clarity, unknotted, knowing the difference between the fact of their nature and how that is reacted to and treated. The trouble is the being back out in the world. It is very hard to always hold those two ropes separate. It is like a gravitational pull to recombine those ropes because the story they are swimming against is so strong. The story that says to be successful in this society you need to be tough, ruthless, strong. It is not a sign of weakness but a sign of strength to attempt to unknot those internal ropes.'

Sitting in the cottage in the dark I realized that that was what was bothering me. An individual HSP can do this work, this unknotting, if they need it. And that can be hugely beneficial, transformative even. But the trouble is, back out in the world, despite them having their ropes unknotted, society still does not react well to or understand their sensitivity. The world still tells them that sensitivity is not valuable, even bad. And therefore it is entirely likely that they become stuck in a never-ending cycle of trying to keep the ropes separate. They are swimming against the current of the society we live in. They are continually locked in a system whereby they must personally acknowledge their own difference in relation to that of the majority and accept that their dominant trait is not held to be of importance, but they then somehow have to find value in that themselves.

I take issue with that. I take real issue with that. I wholly agree with individual work, and I have done a lot of that work myself. But that individual work runs against a narrative with a very strong current. A very strong story about what is of value to the society we live in. That story goes: the things that are of value are competition, strength, boldness, certainty, unquestioned charisma, leadership, fast doing. The strongest succeed. The toughest survive.

I feared for the man at the literary salon who had told me that for him, identifying as highly sensitive had given him back the sun. I feared that his relief was temporary, that he was going to face a disappointing moment post-self-realization, when he discovered society's feeling towards sensitivity. That the onus would be on him to show and to keep showing that he has value. Hearing your own traits understood and explained as an HSP is very rewarding. But I am not sure that HSPs understanding and managing their sensitivity better changes the story. In fact, I think it keeps the same story in place, with HSPs doing all the work to manage themselves. I think we have a problem in our cultural story, one that has profound bias towards who and what has value. It is deeply problematic that one fifth of the population is likely to have experienced being told by social conditioning that they are the wrong shape, have the wrong nature, are lacking value. That is a sign of something bigger than HSPs. It is a sign that we have a society that is in massive trouble.

I do not believe it is valuable to us, any of us, to have individuals sitting in dark rooms doing all the work of unknotting ropes. There is other work to be done. Work concerning the story of who and what we value, who and what we are. We we are living in an era of competition, fast decision-making, time economy, hyperconnectivity, resource threat, opposition. The emphasis within our society on material objects, prioritizing your own needs – to get ahead, to win, to climb up over others if there is gain to be achieved – is palpable. If you google 'values of the 21st century', this is what comes up: diversity, responsibility, community, creativity and innovation. But I think that is idealistic. Those are the ideals we wish we were living, that we should by all rights be living. But we are not. There are, of course, small, exquisite examples of diversity, responsibility, community, creativity and innovation, but in the main we live in a consumerist, capitalist society, and that forms our values and who and what we believe in. We live prioritizing consumption, competition, achievement. We consider a life structured around those values to be a normal life, a normal set of values by which to measure achievement and success. And therein lies the challenge with finding a word or description that sums up what we mean by the opposite of sensitive. If sensitive is one binary – what is its opposite? It's problematic even to try and unpick that.

For example, we label sensitivity as a problem. So does that mean the opposite of sensitive is not a problem – it's normal? Is the opposite of sensitive insensitive? I think that is a little insulting to the 'normal' people. We label sensitivity as weakness, so does that mean the opposite of sensitivity is strength? Ah, I think therein lies the problem. I believe and want to set out to show that sensitivity is, in fact, a much misunderstood strength. And that labelling it as weak, not normal, a problem, undermines its currency, not just for HSPs but for us all. Elaine Aron's research shows us that sensitivity is normal, common even – one in five of us. But we have a biased story, a story of binary opposites – good traits, bad traits, weak, strong, winner, loser. Yet in this story only one half of the binary has a name. So, in the interests of giving the characters in the story names, we need to name the opposite of sensitivity. And the reason for that is because to begin to change anything, it must first be named.

Rebecca Solnit, in her collection of essays *Call Them by Their True Names*, deals with an America in crisis. She does exactly what the title suggests, calls things by their true names – environmental destruction, racism, sexism. She begins the collection with a story about the common folktale of a threatening and mysterious stranger who can only be thwarted when their real name is known. 'Once we call it by its true name, we can start having a real conversation about our priorities and values.'

So, what name to give to the opposite of sensitivity? I have spent a good few years now trying to discover the name of this mysterious stranger. The best I can offer, and I am deeply sorry if this offends, but the best I can offer as the opposite of sensitive is 'sociopath'. Does that do the job? Is our society run by values of sociopathy? T Byram Karasu, one of America's leading professors of psychiatry, illustrates that the age of narcissism has metamorphosed into the more virulent age of sociopathy, where selfishness, greed and the violation of the rights of others have become fixtures of daily life, and where empathy seems to be a dying emotion.

Whatever your views on whether or not sociopathy is the right term, it is helpful in understanding two binaries; sensitivity and sociopathy. Our world is built for sociopaths; we have created a society where the ultimate winners are sociopaths and the ultimate losers are those who are very sensitive. Holding judgement aside on that, it offers us an interesting part of the story – contempt for sensitivity is largely to do with how poorly it manoeuvres in the values of a sociopathic culture. It feels like this is a story of taught tensions, opposite needs. I also understand now, in a much clearer way, that on one hand this book is about HSPs, but it is equally about the traits and values we as a society hold collectively, whether or not those are the right ones. And so, with that set of useful and inflammatory tensions in place between sociopaths and highly sensitive people, I would like to understand the process by which this division develops. What systems keep in place the values by which we live? And why?

Parental emotional expressions towards children have a huge impact upon those children and the story they internally tell about themselves. If I wish my child to have a positive relationship with her sensitivity, then I must learn to develop a truly positive relationship with mine. Otherwise, I am paying it lip service, while emanating concern and possible shame towards my child as she sees herself in me. My talented artist wellbeing therapist Louise Platt believes that shame shifts when you respond to it with curiosity. She describes it as being like bringing a balm to a wound, or something light to something dark. It turns self-statements such as 'I shouldn't be like this' into 'Why am I like this? 'I am weak because I feel too much' becomes 'What are the benefits of feeling a lot?' So, in the name of bringing dark things out into the light, changing our own story of sensitivity, here are some of my more embarrassing examples:

- I take negative things people say straight to heart and somehow keep them as a means to torment myself. I forget the positive.
- I give priority to other people's feelings and needs above my own and don't often say what I want or need.
- I self-doubt a lot, and when reflecting on my actions I will often concede my position, hesitate, retreat and listen to

more certain voices. However, I often feel compromised by the outcome, sometimes resentful.

- I often want to leave group environments suddenly. I once left a mum-and-baby group in a café without saying goodbye to the people I was with or taking the pram which contained the keys to my flat, because I could not stop reading the subtext of the social group. The competitive mums talking over each other about 100 per cent cotton and where to buy ethical avocados were exhausting. No one was talking about anything honest, and I knew I needed to get out of there. I considered simply saying, 'I need to go, bye,' but I did not want to have the awkward conversation about leaving whereby you are then guilt-tripped into staying, and everyone says, 'Oh, such a shame.' So instead I picked up my daughter, excused myself saying I was going to the bathroom, and on the way to the bathroom swerved left out the door. As I said, I did not have the keys to my flat, or the pram, so I walked down back streets around the neighbourhood for forty-five minutes until I was confident they would have left, before returning to collect my things.

- I sometimes even hide at my own social gatherings. Once, as a student at my own house party, after having had a brilliant time, I eventually got exhausted by conversation, lights, music and noise. So I wandered up into the attic bedroom and, finding a pile of the guests' coats, got under them to have a nap. It was so peaceful under there that I did not come out, not even when two people came in and had sex. It seemed rude to disturb them and make them jump by getting up to leave.

- I sometimes find sensory discomforts quite literally unbearable. I once got off a train at the wrong station because

I could not bear the smell of a woman's heavy perfume.

• If I'm uncomfortable with something in a hospitality environment, I will go out of my way not to mention it. I slept on the floor of a B&B because the texture of the bedsheets was too crackly, and when I checked out in the morning and they asked me if everything was OK, I said, 'Yes, wonderful' and gave them a five-star review.

• I find it challenging to say what I want and need because I am concerned about the feelings and wants and needs of the other person. When I got married, I had a dress made. Just a simple dress, long-sleeved, cut under the bust, knee-length, because I have one of those hourglass figures that clothes never fit that well, and I thought, 'Well, on this day of all days it would be nice to have a dress that fits me properly.' Three days before the wedding I went to collect it. The dressmaker said, 'Try it on.' So I did, and looked in the mirror. I think there must have been a miscommunication somewhere along the line; it was very different to what we had discussed. But she looked so excited and hopeful and said, 'Do you love it?' And I was gutted. But I paused, smiled brightly, and said, 'Yes, it's fantastic.' I was devastated. I am not a girly type of person, and I had just so hoped that on this one occasion I might have a nice dress. I sent her some thank-you flowers with a note that read, 'Thank you for taking such care.' And it meant I did not have a wedding dress, but instead a truly disgusting £30 dress from TK Maxx grabbed from a rail two days before the ceremony. I looked awful, felt awful, fully paid for the dress, and said nothing. Didn't want a fuss. Everyone on the wedding day kept rubbing my arm and looking at me pitifully and saying, 'Oh, I am so sorry, it would have been so nice to look nice, wouldn't it?' Mortified.

• I need to observe before participating. When I was three, my mum took me to a music playgroup in a rundown church hall. The hall had blue plastic chairs on metal frames and a sticky varnished floor. When it was time for the class to begin, the group leader said, 'OK, everyone come in and choose an instrument.' All the kids rushed in, into a little hive, and grabbed an instrument. Music was my favourite thing. I spent hours making up elaborate music shows at home. But I refused to go and get an instrument, which meant no participating in the song. Mum says this filled her with anxiety, she just wanted me to fit in. She knew I wanted to take part, but I seemed to need to watch before getting involved, which sometimes meant missing out entirely.

I was ashamed about my daughter doing the same thing as me. When she was three, I took her to a music playgroup in a rundown church hall. The hall had blue plastic chairs on metal frames and a sticky varnished floor. The group leader said, 'OK, guys, come and choose an instrument.' All the kids rushed in, but my daughter did not. And remembering the story my mum had told me, I took hold of her hand and said, 'OK, darling, we are going to go and get an instrument.' But she tensed and hid behind my leg. So, I picked her up, carried her into the middle and said, 'A glockenspiel or a triangle?' and she hid her face in my neck. The group of parents were watching, and I felt hot in the face, so I knelt and said, 'Look, sweetheart, if you don't choose an instrument you cannot join in the song, don't you want to join in the song with everyone?' And she looked around her at the people looking and began to cry. Everyone was watching, so I picked her up and carried her out, not even stopping to put our coats on. Walking home I was angry. She could not be like me;

in fact, I would not let her be like me. So, I sat my three-year-old down on a bench and explained how things are in the world, how she can't opt out of participating, how you have got to get up and out there, to take part first time, otherwise you do not get a space, OK?

And she listened, watching my face, nodded, and said, 'Yes mummy.'

That frustration that I felt towards my child for not engaging in the same way that the other children did was surprising to me. It does not fit at all with my world view or working practice. I catch myself on the shame of that – the second-hand shame, passed down to my mum, to me, and now to my daughter, like an old itchy jumper. Many of us so very much want to be how everyone else is, to engage with things that other people seem to manage so well, rather than feeling, as my mum describes, 'like a brick wall is in front of you all the time'. Why was my child not joining straight in like the other children? Why was I so embarrassed of that and smiling at the other mothers? She was not engaging in the way that we expect, immediate and unquestioning. I knew this behaviour, this observation before participating, and I felt it was not good at all. It felt infinitely familiar, under-the-skin familiar. I felt the prickles of embarrassment from my own childhood, that moment of realizing that you are engaging differently, that you are different, and the panic that comes with that. I have memory upon memory of being in a classroom, workplace, social environment when something is presented for us to engage with: a dance, an experiment, a team-building exercise, a group game. I want to participate, the will is there, but I am rooted hard to the spot. I need to watch first, learn the rules, learn what is expected, how others are going to play, and I am embarrassed by this need. It is not an option to just throw myself in and do it. I just don't work that way. And, it appears, nor does my child.

My daughter is five now, and at parties she still does this. She likes to stand next to the party entertainer and help them hand out props like balloons. She does not want to participate straight away. She will take part in a different way. But standing at the side of village halls, the kids all in the middle of the room trying to catch balloons with their knees, my child helping the entertainer lay out the next activity, I realize how very much she is made of the same stuff that I am, and immediately my parental protectiveness and concern for her rockets. I do not want her to live like me. I do not want her to have my experience. I want her to be in the throng, joining in, not knowing any different, participating joyfully and without question. Pregnant, I had sworn to myself that no matter who our child would be, I would help them find the right conditions to thrive. But there I was echoing my parents', and perhaps my grandparents', worry, the worry that is really a frightened plea – 'Oh, please, let my child find a route through the world and let their own nature not block them, let them not feel that shame.' My beautiful daughter, helping the entertainer lay out bubble wands, while all the other children were doing spooky dancing to 'Ghostbusters', noticed another child start to cry. She stopped, walked over, bent down and said in the same tone I use to soothe her, 'Hey, it's OK, sweetheart, it's OK.' And the mother of that child looked over to me, met my eye, smiled and nodded.

For a lot of us, a large part of the story we have about sensitivity is formed by shame and secrecy, embarrassment and attempts to fit in. I realize that a key point of changing the story is airing some of that stuff out. Embarrassed as I am about those things I have just told you, sharing them helps me to see them in a different way. It helps me to understand and start to accept my sensitivity as a part of myself that need not live in shame.

Saying those things out loud helps me to realize how fundamentally I need to change my approach and understanding in relation to raising a highly sensitive child. I am worried that my worry may unduly influence my child's development and life direction. I want to understand what the trajectory of possibilities is for highly sensitive children. I want to know what the right conditions are for them, and if there are conditions that actively work against them.

3. Somewhere on the scale

To learn more about whether there are better or worse conditions for the highly sensitive, I wanted to talk to Professor Michael Pluess, an educational psychologist, who has collaborated extensively on research with Dr Elaine Aron. I first met Michael in September 2018 for a documentary I was making with producer Giles Edwards for Radio 4. We travelled to London to Michael's office at Queen Mary University of London (QMUL). Upon arriving at QMUL, Giles and I followed a paper map to the department and spent a full fifteen minutes trying to figure out how to get through the swipe-card doors in front of a courtyard of students enjoying the late summer sun. Once in, we started to talk in whispers, because academic, neat, green-carpeted places command a kind of reverence, and together we found Michael's door.

'Knock, Hannah,' said Giles.

'I'm nervous. What if my questions aren't right?' I replied.

'Knock, Hannah,' Giles repeated, taking out the microphone to record the knock for the documentary soundscape. Kind-faced, sandy-haired Michael Pluess opened the door and invited us to sit at his round wooden table, setting down a carafe and water glasses. I began by asking him to introduce himself.

SENSITIVE

Michael: My name is Michael Pluess. I am a Professor of Developmental Psychology, based at Queen Mary University of London. Lots of my research deals with environmental sensitivity, the idea that some people are more affected by what they experience than others.

Hannah: How do you describe sensitivity?

Michael: A basic and common trait, the ability to perceive the environment and process information about it, with the aim of responding as appropriately as possible. It is a capability we can see in lots of species from humans to fish, and even insects.

Hannah: Does everyone have it?

Michael: Yes, everyone is sensitive, but people differ in their level of sensitivity. Some are more and some less sensitive. That's not a new discovery, we have known this for a while, but what we've been able to show in recent years is that sensitive people are not only more likely to be negatively affected by negative experience, but also more likely to be positively affected by positive experience.

If you go online and look at sensitivity information on websites, that information often suggests that there are two groups of people: a small group of highly sensitive ones versus everyone else who is low in sensitivity. It doesn't quite work like that. We found that there are three different groups: low, medium and high. We use flower metaphors for ease. Dandelions are at the lower end of the scale – dandelions are not highly sensitive, they grow well anywhere and make up

48

about 30 per cent of the population. At the opposite end of the scale are orchids – orchids need the right conditions to thrive and also make up about 30 per cent of the population. And in the middle, we have tulips, which make up the remaining 40 per cent of the population.

Importantly, even though there are these three groups, sensitivity is best understood as a continuum from low to high. And sensitivity is not a disorder, not a pathological condition, but a common temperament trait.

Hannah: How early in life does high sensitivity display?

Michael: We found there are clear differences at age three, and the more sensitive children are rated, the more strongly they're affected by the parenting quality they receive.

Hannah: Ha, well that is good to know for me as a parent!

Michael: Those who are most sensitive are at higher risk to develop problems if they receive poor parenting, but also have the least problems if they receive high-quality parenting.

Hannah: Culturally, do you think we see sensitivity as something weaker?

Michael: Probably, yes. Several personality traits are associated with sensitivity, including neuroticism in particular. Generally, neuroticism and introversion have a more negative connotation in our culture. But sensitivity is neither bad nor good in itself. More sensitive people are simply more affected by their environment. Importantly, there are also sensitive extroverts.

Hannah: Why do you think this trait is in us?

Michael: Because it is essential to adapt well to the specific conditions of our environment, to perceive its features, and figure out what we need to do to thrive in our environment. Everyone is sensitive, but some more than others. They have different advantages from low-sensitive people, but having both groups represented in a society is important. There are many positive sides to sensitivity. It is an important trait for many different professions. It's helpful as a therapist, for example. Sensitive people tend to have more empathy, they understand other people more easily. They are good listeners. Often they tend to be artists, scientists, coaches, counsellors. They often have good interpersonal skills, are good at thinking things through, they are not superficial. And highly sensitive people can be very successful if they are able to manage the more challenging aspects of their sensitivity. Our studies show that the sensitive children, in fact, outperform less sensitive children, in a positive environment.

We find many people aren't aware of the differences in sensitivity, and the world is not really set up for highly sensitive people. For example, we assume people are the same, that open-plan offices work for everyone. Schools assume group activities work for everyone. Our work is starting to question whether sensitive children need different classroom setups. They might learn better by themselves rather than in groups.

Hannah: And what type of trait do you think the education system is currently set up to favour?

Michael: I would say less sensitive children.

Hannah: Michael, where are you on the sensitivity scale?

Michael: I've tested myself. I'm at the higher end of the tulip group. This may be a reflection of me being highly sensitive but growing up in a supportive environment.

Hannah: People seem to often confuse high sensitivity with autism because of the sensory sensitivity.

Michael: Yes, but sensitivity and autism are very different things. Sensitivity is not a disorder, but a common trait. And highly sensitive people are particularly good in relational matters, in contrast to many people on the autistic spectrum. The overlap between sensitivity and autism is mostly due to shared sensory sensitivity, such as a strong response to bright lights, etc. There are some commonalities, but both are quite different.

Speaking with Professor Michael Pluess radically changed my understanding of sensitivity. He explained that it is a basic and common trait. He described it in not dissimilar language to Robin Skeates – as simply a way of processing the world.

Talking to Professor Pluess also changed how I felt about sensitivity – truly for the first time in handling the subject, I did not feel that talking about it was shameful. His pragmatism was useful in getting some of the facts pinned in place. Sensitivity is neither bad nor good. It is neutral. I can live with that. I find that helpful.

Professor Pluess's work also overturned a part of the story I thought we had arrived at in the last chapter – the idea that sensitivity is binary, that there are sociopaths and HSPs. Instead, there is a scale and we are all somewhere on that scale. That gives a much more rounded and comprehensive understanding. We are a variable species. I enjoy the articulation that Professor Pluess used of 'more sensitive children' and 'less sensitive children'. It really focused for me that sensitivity is something in all of us, just in different degrees. That understanding helps me to feel at peace with articulating out loud that my child and I sit at one end of a scale of sensitivity. It feels much less like being branded, and much more like explaining the diversity of us all.

The explanation that sensitivity is valuable because it offers us the ability to usefully perceive our environment and process information about it with the aim of responding as well as possible blew my mind. Of course that is the value of sensitivity! Appropriate response. The more you observe and consider, the more likely it is that you will offer an appropriate response to a person or situation. It seems obvious to me now, that piece of value, with the arrogance of hindsight. But that is a radical new thought, that those who are more sensitive are possibly better at offering an appropriate response, and that observing before participating is an extension of that. It felt nourishing and a little emotional to hear the positives of HSPs in concrete language: more empathy, better listeners, good interpersonal skills, good at thinking things through. Key building blocks of a better story for sensitivity: it is a common basic trait, neither good nor bad, we are all on a scale, HSPs are particularly good at empathy, listening, interpersonal skills, thinking things through.

I was also struck by Professor Pluess's reflection that highly sensitive children are more likely to be affected by both a negative and a positive environment, reminding me of one of the reasons I had interviewed him in the first place – my concern about the impact of my worry on my highly sensitive child. A negative environment can constitute all sorts of things, from horrific to mild, and though parental emotional leaking is far from the most severe, it still has a significant impact on a child's view of their own self-worth. But if it is touching to learn and reframe your own childhood experiences, to shift your own narrative, to be doing that work as an adult, then it is sobering to remember you may well be the care provider for someone made of similar stuff. In my life; my daughter.

It feels tremendously uplifting to know that, with the right conditions, it is more than possible for highly sensitive children to hugely succeed – even to out-succeed others. But with the right conditions ... That can mean so many things – the right story you are told about yourself, the type of learning environment you are in, the right kind of friends and partners and jobs. These are all important. I believe these are all formed by the big cultural story we live in. So, what is the story we collectively live inside? What story of worth do we tell? One of social norms, of ethical values, of an individual's value in relation to productivity, net worth and success in the job economy. We tell a story of easy fitting, instant engagement, overriding our supposed weak parts in order to succeed. A story of fast decision-making, no hesitation, charismatic leaders; of the success of the supposed strongest – and that has a massive impact. It shapes the world we live in. We admire those values, teach them, the job market asks for them. Our emotional response to things is not something high up in our value system, nor are professions with care at their centre, such as nursing. Yes, we value them in the abstract, we value them when they are there caring for those we love, but we don't match that value in terms of salaries. Sensitivity is thought of as something good to use when needed, but not of necessary value. It is considered inconvenient, surplus, messy. Our soft underbelly. Nice that it is there, but not a priority.

What that means is that the society we live in is created in the model of the values we subscribe to, our dominant values. As Professor Pluess said, the world is not really set up for highly sensitive people. It assumes, for convenience, that there is a one-size-fits-all learning and working environment – open-plan offices, group activities at school. I am going to repeat that. The world is not really set up for highly sensitive people. I had to let that sit for a while, to digest. It felt good to hear it, a sort of relief. Because no one tells an HSP that the world is not really set up for their needs: what you are told is that the world is set up just fine for everyone else, but you do not fit. If you are sensitive, then the odds are stacked against you. What that means is that, to succeed, a highly sensitive person either needs to have lucked out with the right conditions – not a privilege afforded to all – or they need to learn to change themselves to fit a system that is not the right shape for them. It is not easy to fit a system that is not designed for you. It is exhausting, it is demoralizing.

Talking to Professor Pluess, I was struck by the measured, considered, curious humanity that he brings to his work and research. I am moved that there are people out there committed to researching how we learn in our diversity and variance, what works for different intelligence types. I feel comforted, like I can say to my younger self, struggling at school, 'Hey, Hannah, look, give it twenty years or so and there will be people who look at these differences, these needs – we will have new understandings, soon.' That helps me be at peace with the past and hopeful for the future.

Talking to Professor Pluess also helped significantly to convert my understanding of sensitivity from 'to be sensitive is to be weak and to struggle' to 'with the right conditions you can excel'.

The fact that sensitivity only really becomes a problem if your conditions actively work against you must mean that we have many successful, high-functioning, highly sensitive people who perhaps do not even determine themselves as such because they had the right conditions to thrive. So the highly sensitive people who are visible are potentially those who have struggled and/or are struggling with their own natures. That probably contributes to giving sensitivity some bad press, and I have no doubt that is part of the cause of its negative connotations.

I wanted to speak to the person who began all the thinking regarding HSPs – who indeed coined the term – about sensitivity and its negative reputation. When I began research for this book, the very first thing I did was to email Dr Elaine Aron. She is the font of all our original understandings regarding HSPs, the queen of HSPs. She is also, however, an incredibly busy and successful professional and has a PA in place to catch the numerous asks addressed to her. I sent three emails asking different questions but could not get past the gate. Then one sweltering summer's afternoon, I thought, just give it another try – I am that kind of person; you never know, just ask. So, I emailed her, asking if she knew of any research regarding sensitivity and evolution. The words I had put in the email worked like a magic key in a lock – she emailed me back! She had agreed to be interviewed.

Hannah: I think it's extraordinary that there's this percentage of the population who can have this amazing power, and now this understanding of their own natures. But what's problematic is that they are still expected to fit into a world that is not right for who they are.

Elaine: Naturally everything is set up for the people who are the 70 per cent, much like the world is set up for the right-handed, but this is a bigger difference than handedness, and we humans have a very hard time seeing two groups as equal. We always look down on or up to a minority group. That must change.

Hannah: I can see that in HSPs being paid less for their work and receiving less respect, and I think that's a waste.

Elaine: That is true, but we must consider that maybe the sensitive people who are most noticed, in the workforce for example, are often those who, due to the differential susceptibility of all highly sensitives, have suffered from a negative past (usually a difficult childhood). That can make them more anxious, depressed, shy or unable to take criticism well. They often feel like victims. I'm sorry for them, deeply. Everyone notices their 'sensitivity', and it creates something of a stereotype, that all HSPs are that way.

Meanwhile, no one notices the sensitive people who are what we might call higher functioning. Due to the same differential susceptibility, they gained more from a positive past (good parents, teachers, etc.) than other children would have. These HSPs are seen in a very positive light – creative, thoughtful, deep and so on – but no one would think of them as 'highly sensitive'. These HSPs who have had supportive childhoods or done their inner work are blending in, adapting to the environment. Only those closest to them would see, for example, that they are easily overstimulated or have strong emotional reactions. You don't see them, but they're accomplishing a lot. Companies may be full of them, and I presume they are paid well, although they tend to be less pushy in that regard. But again, no one is thinking of them as sensitive. Every sensitive person can be there. It's just a matter of some therapy or other work on oneself, and the good news is that, again due to differential susceptibility, we get more from positive interventions like that than less sensitive people do. So, there's no reason not to just go to work on oneself and fix these things that are a problem.

It was a great privilege to talk to Dr Elaine Aron; she has helped so many HSPs. Reading through the interview I thought, yes, I bet there are many successful HSPs out there in the world, who we don't notice particularly, those who have had good variables in their childhoods, who are understood as creative, thoughtful, who perhaps only in private share their deep emotions. Yes, HSPs who struggle are, of course, much more visible, and that contributes to sensitivity having a negative story. That makes me feel deeply uncomfortable. If it works for you and you are lucky enough to get the right conditions, then there is relative silence around the trait that has helped you succeed. But if you are not lucky enough to get the right conditions, then it is likely you will struggle. And if you speak up about struggling, you are likely to be told, well, the only people who struggle are the weak ones. That's not fair, it's not just. And I think, also, possibly not true. But what it produces is an excuse, an excuse for us collectively to ignore the trait of sensitivity. It gives us a reason to problematize and deprioritize it. It is kept in place with a story of shame and an act of complicity.

There are so many parts of our society that we keep quiet like this, narratives not heard, considered not as important, not as central to human experience. I remember very clearly after the birth of my daughter wanting to talk about the birth experience. I was so lucky to have had a great experience, I wanted to be able to say, 'Mate, do you have any idea what I managed to do? I am amazing, I can walk through fire.' I couldn't believe that this is how we all get here, that it is so painful and so hard, and yet the species is so very here, and there are so many of us. I wanted to talk about the significance of birth, what it means, what it changes, how we each manage, the fact that we can. I just found it extraordinary. I remember during labour two Scottish nurses saying, 'OK, put your feet on our hips and push like your life depends on it.'

'No,' I said, 'I will hurt you, I can't push against your body.'

'Yes, you can,' one of them said. 'We are stronger than we look.'

I cannot forget that kindness, the conviction I gained from them that this was something I could do, that they were going to help me to do it. But I found post-birth that it was not socially acceptable to discuss it. Men squeamed away from the conversation, women were complicated, raising generational stories, warning stories, passive-aggressive stories of luck and worth. A friend said to me, 'It's a silenced narrative. Know why? If you say you had a good birth it is considered boasting. If you say you did not have a good birth it is considered scaremongering.' And I think that is true: the story of birth, how every single one of us gets into this world, is not generally talked about, or rather it is kept in little gendered silos. And so, we have generations of shocked new mothers: 'Why didn't anyone tell me?' Damned if you do, damned if you don't.

I use that as an example because othered narratives like that signify a problem with a system of values, permission, space taking, who gets heard, who gets prioritized, what stories we tell.

And if that can happen with half the population – women – it's easy for it to happen with one fifth of the population – HSPs. I wonder again, what keeps in place the poor conditions that (in the main) prevent HSPs from thriving? Why do the successful HSPs – people who had the right conditions, and are highly emotionally intelligent, thoughtful, quiet leaders – why do they not understand their success as being due in large part to the trait of sensitivity? What is going on there?

I wonder how many people do not fit the system we live in, how many types of intelligence and traits. I wonder what the real statistics are. We are told the system suits 70 per cent of people. I wonder if it is much less. I understand that we need a system that is easy to implement, that is clear and efficient and standardized. But I feel disappointed that we have a one-size-fits-all system – and it is clear from societal psychological studies that that is what we do have. The responsibility to change oneself, to learn to fit, currently sits with the highly sensitive person, even though this radical research is being done into environment. The story is that the system won't change; you need to. No matter how long I spend with this subject, I just can't get over how many people that affects. The system is not set up for one fifth of the population. Are we all right with that? Collectively, do we think that is OK? Do we think, well, it's not me who doesn't fit? I think a lot of us do have that thought – until it is our child, our friend, our partner; suddenly then we have a vested interest.

I wonder if the four fifths who are well suited to the system are aware of the privilege of not struggling. I realize I am angry writing this. I am not angry at myself for not fitting in – I have done those days – and I am not angry at those who do fit – not their fault. I am angry at the system of values we collectively keep and live in, seemingly without challenge or question. I wonder:

do people only change things if they affect them personally? That is... shit. If that is the case, then let's look at whether the system is in fact suiting those four fifths of the population. How everything is working out. How would we know?

Well, I don't think it's hard to see that societally, individually, collectively, we are struggling in a wide variety of directions. If you look at the news, you will see a series of disruptions, collapses, compromised systems, catastrophes. Things are not looking good, for any of us. It's worse than that – things are looking catastrophic. And what are we doing in response? Are we reacting appropriately? Which means; what are we doing about it? Have we appropriately considered what to do next? How we are we working together on a large scale to change it? I think that what we are doing is keeping the same old systems in place, in the main, like running on the spot. The messaging is, the system won't change, you need to. Why? What if that messaging is fundamentally wrong? What if the system works for none of us anymore?

I want us to explore an example of a system we keep in place without significantly changing it to meet the appropriate conditions. The education system is built to suit 70 per cent of the population, the majority. It is there to equip our future workers with the skills needed to fuel the job economy, to create citizens. I have twenty-two years' experience working in education across a very broad range of settings. And yes, I am passionate about education and its values, but I also think it is a good working example of where we are at in terms of our relationship to a changing environment.

4. We are what we teach

I have an interest in education – actually, what I find
is everybody has an interest in education...it's one of
those things that goes deep with people, am I right?
Like religion, and money, and other things. I have
a big interest in education, and I think we all do.
We have a huge, vested interest in it, partly because
it's education that's meant to take us into this future
that we can't grasp.
SIR KEN ROBINSON

Yes, dear late Sir Ken, education runs deep for us all – no matter
what your experience. And what is interesting about education
is that though it is deeply personal, we all have a vested interest
in it because it is the skills learned in the education system that
are going to help us face 'this future that we can't grasp'. Our
young rise to inherit the world shaped by previous generations
– for better or worse. We all need our young to emerge from the
education system with the skills to support a future economy, or
we don't have a functional future economy. So yes, education is
about you, but it is also about us all, and the system we all live
and survive in.

Education is the root of us, where we learn skills, knowledge, socializing, our specific value as an individual. School is the place where we begin to teach children how they will fit and find their place in the world, it's one of the main places we develop our sense of self.

So how do we educate? Well, to answer that is another whole book. But to understand what we would call a pinnacle example of a good education, we need to look to our prime privileged education, a private school education. In August 2021, the *Guardian* published an article by Richard Beard called 'Why Public Schoolboys Like Me and Boris Johnson Aren't Fit to Run Our Country'. In it, Beard explained that at an elite boarding school, emotional austerity is taught as a matter of course:

> We could cry if we liked but no one would help us. So later in life, when we saw people cry, we felt no great need to go to their aid. The sad and weak were wrong to show their distress, and so we learned to despise the children who blubbed for their mummies.

The article went on to quote psychoanalyst Joy Schaverien's book *Boarding School Syndrome*, explaining a condition that develops from such treatment. The symptoms include 'emotional detachment and dissociation, cynicism, exceptionalism, defensive arrogance, offensive arrogance, cliquism, compartmentalization, guilt, grief, denial, strategic emotional misdirection and stiff-lipped stoicism', all of which are, according to Schaverien, 'ingrained from an early age'.

This is what we hold up as the golden model of education, the image in which we build the rest of the system. This is where we elect our leaders from. It goes quite a long way to explaining our relationship to sensitivity – it is taught in public schools as a thing to be educated out of, and that filters down.

I regularly work in schools as a writing workshop leader. I get to go into a very wide range of learning establishments, from Pupil Referral Units to young carers, from kids in psychiatric care to gifted and talented students, and everyone in between. School environments are not one-size-fits-all, for better or for worse: they each have their own character and atmosphere, you can tell what is of value to a school from so many things: is the work on the wall all perfect, or is there variety within it? Is the classroom too neat? Has the children's play been tidied out? How does the teacher address their students? Who puts up their hand? Which children or staff hold themselves with confidence, meet your eye, talk to you in the staff room? Schools are pressured places, with endless standards placed on them by external agencies, and they achieve extraordinary acts of endurance and brilliance. As an outsider, you can learn so much about the values of a school just by sitting in the staff room or waiting in reception.

Schools each have their own character and values, you can see that sloganned across every school – things like 'Our values are community, bravery, inclusivity.' But collectively, schools are held to account by measuring their output and governance in relation to a standardized system that is held in place by a set of agreed values and aims, set from above. For example, there currently isn't an option not to prioritize individual pupil achievement: the shape of the curriculum, the shape of the year is geared towards repeated exam-taking. Schools work to get their pupils to pass exams, not to break the law, to be useful citizens. But above even the importance of citizenship, exams and output rule supreme.

I want to take a minute to make it crystal clear that I am continuously humbled by the commitment, empathy and resilience of teaching staff. Teachers are in the main extraordinary people, up there with the very highest order of humans. Many of us have had that single extraordinary teacher who went the extra mile for us, who understood us and what we could be – mine was my English teacher Mrs Smith. It's because of her that I went to university, and without that I would not have become a writer. There are individual schools run with radical leadership, pupil-led learning, prioritizing a diversity of learning preferences. There are schools with incredible values that they manage to implement and instil in their pupils and communities. But in the main, I do not believe this to be the case. Those rare schools are the result of specific individuals inspiring and creating communities of change, working against the current. They are not the norm. And the norm is very worrying.

What is school for? To enable us to get a job. To be a useful member of society. To supply the economy with future skilled workers. Childcare. Those are the most common answers you will get if you ask. But school is more – while at school we are exposed to a system of values, a way of thinking, a set of priorities. This experience significantly shapes each one of us. The process of school is one that brings together a group of children with assorted traits and skills and trains them to think and act in a particular way. Throughout the process of education, traits and skills are sorted into a hierarchy. School is for education, and by that we mean more than just the information taught. What is an education? Einstein is often said to have defined it as 'what remains after one has forgotten everything he learned in school'. Some of the content we learn in school is very useful. Quite a lot is not. It is an exercise in learning how to learn, learning how to conform, learning how to jump hurdles. What we are learning in school is an understanding of how the world works, it is 'how to be in the world' training. It is supposed that within the education system is a system of values that clearly tally with and reflect how the world works. So, what are those values? What world are we preparing children for? What skills are needed for being in the world now?

To dig underneath whether the system and the world are in synthesis, I wanted to interview someone senior within the Department for Education, because they make massive decisions about what children are taught, what skills are needed in the job economy and so forth. They were very busy though, you know, educating people, and did not get back to me in terms of an interview. I did receive one email saying we do not understand why you would want to have a conversation about what values are behind the education system, but we can talk to you about curriculum content. Entirely missing the point. So, as an alternative, I contacted an extraordinary organization I have had the privilege of being trained by – The Map Consortium, specialists in creative facilitation and training. They kindly responded saying that they knew the Right Honourable Lord Knight of Weymouth, former Labour Education and Employment Minister, and now a consultant adviser to education companies – would that do? Er, yeah, it would, thanks. I wasn't expecting to be able to speak to someone quite so senior and informed – I was beyond thrilled and grateful.

We had this conversation on a sunny day in spring 2021, at the tail end of lockdown two, when people were venturing out of their houses for the first time in a long time and everyone had that look on their face of wanting to grab and hug the nearest stranger as proof of their existence and proximity. Setting up the camera and recording equipment, I realized I was nervous. I had never met a peer before, so I sat and counted down the minutes.

I wouldn't recommend that as a calming technique. He began the interview in the way a lot of truly powerful people do, by talking about inconsequential things, establishing a rapport by talking about walking routes and what you had for breakfast. Then, in a flash, we moved right into the heart of my favourite topic – education.

———————

Jim: Hello, my name is Jim Knight, I am the Right Honourable Lord Knight of Weymouth, former Education and Employment Minister and now consultant adviser to education companies.

Hannah: Jim, what are the values that the education system is built on?

Jim: These are just my views, OK?

Hannah: Yes, I'd like to hear your views.

Jim: I'm of the view, and I'm not alone, that the education system is constructed based on the needs of our elite universities and acts as a great filtering tool for academic institutions. To understand what values education is based on now, you must understand why it was developed, its context.

So, to offer a super-short potted history: the system moved from learning largely being done via the master apprenticeship model into university for all. At first, university was really something for priests, then it became something for other forms of scholar. You didn't go to university to go around the world, or to run countries or companies. Then the Industrial

Age happened, and the social reformers realized that sending kids up chimneys and into factories was not successful or good. Schooling then moved into something offered until age fourteen and had the function of literally schooling people to get them to turn up on time, to do what they were told, and to read and write so that functionally they were able to conform to what was needed to work in factories. Within that schooling system there was some selection along the way to find the top 10 per cent, who went to university. And then, after the Second World War, education shifted enough to give universal provision in terms of education up to age sixteen for all.

When I went to school, the number of people getting to go to university was still about 13 per cent. My dad was an accountant. He never had a degree, because you could enter professions other ways, such as through articles. And since then, we've seen this big widening of access to university, and that's driven school policy here. The system was designed on the basis that if you failed your O-levels [the precursor of GCSEs], you were probably still left with at least a few, so you were functionally literate and numerate, and with those you could get a job in a factory and still have a reasonably secure income.

As the economy has shifted and society has developed, we've not shifted that education system. What we have done is widen access to universities in the hope that that will deliver more social mobility. And the government ambition of 'Let's get 50 per cent of the school output to go to university', which we never quite managed to hit, well, that was still going to leave 50 per cent without the option of a factory job and without security of work in an economy that is now moving to a requirement for everyone essentially to have higher levels of skill, because machines can do more and more.

So we know we are at a point where we need to really shift the system. We need to shift away from it being a system of 'Let's set a number of tests as obstacles to measure academic prowess.' We are the most tested nation in the world, we spend around two or three billion a year in our schools on tests, and huge amounts of effort. And why? There are very successful jurisdictions around the world that only have statutory public examinations at school when they leave aged eighteen.

Is it possible for us to have that? It produces a more rounded person, and allows for other types of intelligence. There is a Holy Grail for education, where we start to wrap schooling around individuals rather than training pupils to conform and accepting that a proportion will fail. A good teacher sees the attributes of each member of their class.

Hannah: Do you feel schools have not shifted to meet the needs of the society as it has changed?

Jim: No, they have not. We even have a system in our public education whereby GCSE and A-levels are designed so that a proportion will fail. To avoid grade inflation, a certain proportion need to not succeed. So we are therefore deciding that certain people are going to fail, and because of that they will probably always be disproportionately disadvantaged. So we have a system that is designed to entrench disadvantage.

Right now, schools are realizing how vital the emotional and social elements of educational environments are in a post-pandemic world. We're worried about the academic catch-up, when we should be worrying about the social and emotional catch-up, so that we can balance cognitive, emotional, social and physical development. That should be the priority.

Hannah: What skills do you think are needed to face an unknown future?

Jim: At the heart of where we need to go is a mindset shift. We need emotionally, socially, physically and intellectually intelligent people. I have been working on that recently on a macro scale. The World Economic Forum did a good piece of work on the competences for the Fourth Industrial Revolution, but here I am mostly referring to the OECD 2030 Competency Review. What stands out for me is the place that they put agency at the heart of this. It's the north point of the compass that everything points towards. You can't predict what the jobs of the future will be, but you can predict it will be a highly fluid environment where individuals are likely to have to change careers several times in their life, and it will be essential that they can deal with excessive amounts of change, and so they need to above all feel empowered around change. Feel that change is something that they can control and put their arms around and steer in their own direction. That's missing massively in education, and we have a health crisis where as many as one in six of our young people have identifiable mental health needs. Agency over change offers one power. We need to be teaching children a balance of conformity, yes, but also the ability to challenge. To be socially successful you do need to know how to conform, mainly. But we also need people who know how to usefully challenge. How to hold those two things together.

Hannah: I wonder if there are other skillsets that are latently within humans that the education system has not valued, that may become useful as the system changes. I think we need to rediversify our understanding of intelligence traits and their uses.

Jim: Yes, indeed. You have made me think of another book that I've recently read, in which the language is beautiful: *English Pastoral* by James Rebanks. He is a hill farmer in Cumbria, and that book also explores skills diversity, but through agricultural practices.

His grandad had become a farmer and farmed the land the way it had been done for quite a long time, with a strong sensitivity to the impact on the land, the diversity of nature and their custodianship of the land as part of an ecosystem. But then economics just went in a different direction during the second half of the 20th century, and it became highly mechanized, and lots of farmers became, by necessity, desensitized to the need for diversity.

And now farmers are having to quickly rediscover the old skills, because the soil is depleted and they are realizing that you cannot think of the land just in terms of balance sheets and spreadsheets, or it's night-night for the environment and our food systems.

Hannah: That is a beautiful metaphor for humanity's wider skillset. That we have mined skills from humanity for a period, and now reached a point of realization that in order to continue with the best chance against the problems we face, such as environmental catastrophe, we need to learn to revalue and nourish the biodiversity of ourselves and our variety of available skills, to understand and distribute value to it as an ecosystem.

Jim: If you want to build a successful business over the long term you must think, 'OK, how do we create a mindset shift in leadership, which says actually we need to be a proper listening organization that listens to everyone?' And create not only an environment, but an infrastructure that means that voices are heard from across the organization, allow those ideas to grow the organization, to use that innovation. Therefore, leadership becomes about enabling rather than directing. But I don't know how long it will take for the education system to realize that, that the system of command and control is a hangover anomaly, and to stop looking and valuing only attainment.

Hannah: I wonder what it would take for the education system to radically change?

Jim: In the end, parents need to want it to change. Because parents vote, and the decisions are made by politicians, and politicians respond to voters. I think it will be interesting to see whether an effect of the pandemic is parents realizing their children's education is not quite fit for purpose. The pandemic has shown parents what their child's learning looks like, and quite a few of them are thinking, 'What the hell is a fronted adverbial, and why does my child need to learn that?' You can imagine them looking at the nature of the learning, the prescription, and thinking, 'Surely our children are more than this?'

Employers need to really push and say, 'Look, yes, of course we need people who can read and write, but more than anything we need people who are just good functioning humans.' We can get machines to remember knowledge and do repetitive tasks. But what we cannot get machines to do well is innovate, to understand human interpersonal relationships, and that's how we create new value. We need socially, emotionally intelligent people as well as intellectually intelligent people.

At one of the organizations I worked for we had some external people come in and look at our dynamic, at us as a team, to maximize our skills. And the big reflection was that we were missing deliberative thinking – we had lots of doers. It's interesting where power sits. The job of good leadership is to listen and observe.

———————

It was a bit of a dream come true to be able to speak to someone who really understands the construction of the system from an aerial view, what is held in place and why. These conversations so often get bogged down in the content of what children are taught. It was incredibly powerful to hear someone with such knowledge say yes, this system is fundamentally flawed, it is not moving with the times, it potentially is not equipping the future with the skills that are needed.

I think Lord Knight is correct: the pandemic and the struggle of home schooling have given parents the time to see inside their child's learning and to wonder, 'Does my child need to know what a fronted adverbial is?' We all know we have a young generation in dire mental health crisis. GPs are prescribing antidepressants for children as young as six. Almost 65,000 young children in the UK are on antidepressants, and that figure is on the rise. Our young are having a very hard time, they are terrified by the world they see in front of them, and they are tested and tested and tested. Subjects being cut and squeezed are the arts, which have been shown to help with mental health and wellbeing as well as a different understanding of skills and identity. And though I am not directly talking about sensitivity, these value choices and structures have huge impact upon the valuing of sensitivity, indeed upon the valuing of anything in real terms that is not results driven. And that is interesting, because as I mentioned previously, the function of education is to provide useful citizens of the future. We do not know what skills will be useful in the future. It may well be that skills such as sensitivity are incredibly valuable to future generations. But currently, those are skills we systematically educate out.

Lord Knight compared the concept of an agricultural ecosystem to an ecosystem of human skills and intelligence. The idea that we have overmined particular skills and intelligences and that there is an emergent need to rediversify is one I completely agree with. Sensitivity is but one trait, one type. What I see when I work in schools are children in a stunning technicolour range of intelligence types and skills – they are so beautiful. Then they are frog-marched into a one-size-fits-all system. I get why that has happened for the last few hundred years – it was useful, it was useful to industrialism, a system that required obedience and conformity, a specific set of skills.

But is that still true? The jobs that the original system was designed to feed, in large part, no longer exist. What we understand to be a job has fundamentally shifted and continues to shift – there is now no such thing as a job for life. But the system of education and values we teach has not significantly shifted, it has made small wriggling concessions, temporary governmental programmes.

I used to work for a government programme, a Labour initiative called Creative Partnerships. It was a national programme with regional hubs and I was in the Norfolk hub. We worked each year with forty-five schools, those who self-identified a need, a challenge in their learning environment. We helped them to identify and articulate that need. Then we collaboratively figured out an experiment to go about exploring it. That would often require the hiring of professionals to come in and work with the staff or pupils. For example, a school might say, we struggle with boys reading past age seven. So we might employ an author and a scientist, who collaborated to create the arrival of an alien pod in the playground. In order to solve the puzzle of what the pod is, pupils might be required to read the next chapters of a book.

Another example might be, our staff are so stressed that it causes tension between them. We might choose to bring in meditation specialists or implement a staff yoga class. The project was there to explore the conditions of education, to help schools self-solve difficulties that seemed insurmountable through conventional means.

That project was ridiculously successful. Then, as soon as there was a change in government, it was stopped in its entirety. In fact, it was sold wholesale to Germany, where it was implanted as part of mainstream education. It is not that no work has taken place to change anything, it is that there have been no significant changes in structural value.

What are the main things we are teaching? Our pupils are now the most tested in the world – is that giving them the skills needed to fit the future economy? Is that giving them the experience and opportunity to emerge from the system as socially rounded, flexible human beings, able to put their arms around change? Because we badly need a future generation that is change-resilient. The system of education is held in place by a set of ideas about what types of people and skills are of use and value. Within that system, sensitivity is othered. Yet ironically, sensitivity is a skill that helps teach change-resilience. And there are many other skills that are deprioritized as a result of this old system. Education is badly in need of a considerable remake. But as Lord Knight said, that won't happen unless employers or parents ask for it, by considering who and what they vote for. A stark reminder of the power and importance of our vote.

Skills that are likely to be useful for the future economy are adaptability, innovation, collaboration, empathy, interpersonal skills, as well as academic achievement and conformity. You will often hear schools say that they understand that, but then it comes to exams and the fact is that they are held so accountable to statistics, they have to just get the herd up and over the fence again and again. That comes at a cost – it shifts the dominant values such as competition and academic achievement into being more important than other skills. In fact, in times of societal crisis, such as the pandemic, subjects such as the arts are thrown overboard first, because the most important thing is that children pass the tests. We teach children that they are silos that need to achieve. That they are the sum total of their individual achievement, that life is a competition. I am curious about the impact upon children's self-worth in general, and even more so if they are among skillset groups that do not fit within this box.

I have had the conversation about the prioritizing of competition in education many times with many educational specialists. There are many who believe competition to be benign, natural, fun, useful. But competition, if over-focused on, has larger implications for society. American educational expert Alfie Kohn states that:

When we set children against one another in contests – from spelling bees to awards assemblies to science 'fairs' (that are really contests), from dodge ball to honour rolls to prizes for the best painting or the most books read – we teach them to confuse excellence with winning, as if the only way to do something well is to outdo others.

As a species, we are collectively facing massive problems, problems that cannot be solved by competition, by solo achievement alone. We have a job market in a dramatically fast process of change. I want to ask – can we afford to keep the values of the education system the same? Isn't that a short-sighted luxury? In the meantime, by keeping in place the system as is, what are we losing? What are we squandering? Human talent, skill, diversity of intelligence. As Lord Knight said, we are in huge need of confident, emotionally intelligent, innovative people, just as much as we need competitive test-acers. But above all else we need a future generation truly prepared to put their arms around change. They are a generation being passed the biggest problem humanity has ever faced. They are being given the most uncertain terrain. It is a disservice to them, to us all, to teach them skills that were useful 200 years ago at the cost of other more appropriate skills. This is not new understanding. Sir Ken Robinson – the international adviser on education I quoted at the start of this chapter – was talking about this twenty years ago, but we have not significantly changed. I think this is outrageous. Sensitivity is one example of a trait and skill systematically deprioritized in the education system; there are many others. I fear that we will not have the diversity of skills and traits we need to face our changing future.

I am married to a research archaeologist who works for Cambridge University. Research archaeologist means he researches more often than he digs. Part of living with an archaeologist involves domestic conversations about past civilizations:

———————

Me: When the Vikings left, what did they leave behind?

My husband: They left behind their DNA, Hannah. We are all Viking. They didn't leave – that is just an idea we have.

———————

That kind of chat. What I have learned from these conversations is that societies have lived and died by their capacity to embrace change or not. And when I think about that skill, the skill to embrace change, I realize that underneath the capacity to embrace change is the skill of sensitivity. To notice something is changing, you need to be sensitive to what is going on around you, you need to be able to notice, listen. To make change happen, you need empathy, cooperation, group action, communication, appropriate response. Are we using that skill? Are we educating out that skill? Sitting here considering the answer, a chill runs across my back.

Just in case you are not on board and believe us to value all learning types and traits equally, I shall offer you a working example of an educational experience. Because I have myself to hand, I am going to use my own experiences. There is nothing special about my educational experiences, I think they are pretty run of the mill, except that I went to a lot of schools – that doesn't happen to everyone. I was average academically, neither good nor bad. No real stand-out skills. But I really struggled with the environment of school, the values, the hierarchy, the culture of play, the competition. I found the rigidity and injustice of school a real challenge. I would see teachers behaving badly, something that was not as measured then as it is now, and I would be filled with rage. I found making friends excruciating. I wanted real friendships that I could trust. I was repeatedly so bamboozled at the musical-chair game of surface friendship. I just didn't fit in. At any school.

Aged eight, after a series of rough schooling experiences involving a lot of physical violence from fellow pupils that I had kept quiet about for a long time, and relentless and complicated emotional taunting, my parents sent me to a child psychologist in Cambridge, in a leafy building with a black iron balcony and a box of tissues by a comfortable chair. The therapist told me that at the weekends she took flamenco classes, and I imagined her in a dramatic, red-layered dress stamping the ground in time to castanets. She was a good therapist, creative in her toolkit, and her empathy made me want to cry, but there is no way I would cry. I had learned by then that the best survival strategy was to bury my sensitivity, hide it at all costs. I was damned if anyone would see me cry. I remember her saying to me, 'I think, Hannah, you have a very low opinion of yourself. I think you have persuaded yourself to hide who you are, I think you are sensitive, and I can help you see that it is OK to be sensitive. Let's do some work on that, OK?'

She asked me to close my eyes and imagine making a big cake. Into it she asked me to add ingredients of things that I liked about myself. There was a big, long silence.

'Let's keep stirring the cake, Hannah,' I remember her saying, 'keep thinking, what do you like about yourself? Even small things.'

Eventually I said, 'I like reading a lot, the characters stay alive in my mind even after the book is over. So can I put in that I like reading? And I know when people are upset, I look after them. Can I add that?'

She agreed. She talked me through imagining the cake being baked and taking it out of the oven to cool, then icing it. And looking at the finished cake and holding in mind, 'These are the things that make me have value. This cake is me.'

At that point, I told her that it was an ugly, pointless cake, 'because noticing when people are upset and liking reading are not good – they are not useful for anything.' I remember some of this exchange, and some of it I found written in a report in my parents' attic, a report written by the child psychologist. Aged eight, I had a low opinion of myself, and this was not because of my home life, which, as I mentioned earlier, was embracing of sensitivity. I am not telling you that in the hope that you will feel sorry for me. I don't feel sorry for myself: it's just that that was my experience, and it is not a rare one. It is a common experience for highly sensitive children who may not have the right conditions. It is a story of systematically not fitting. So, just a bit about that experience:

What I needed
- **The opportunity to observe before participating in activity.** Engagement at school is fast and decisive. Who knows the answer? Hands up. Who wants to do this activity? Hands up. I did want to do those things, but I would be rooted to the spot, not out of shyness, but out of a crucial need to watch how the activity went first, to understand what was being asked. This was often interpreted as shyness (which I am not) or obstinacy (I am also not). Classrooms are run with compliance and immediacy in mind. I never spoke in class, right the way through to the end of my degree at university.

This annoyed teachers sometimes and I knew that, and I fretted about it, so not only did I not participate but I then shame-spiralled about it. And felt separate from the rest of the class – an outsider, a non-participator. I interpreted this as being a loser.

- **Paired working or solo where possible.** At the schools I went to, group working was relentlessly pushed on us, day in, day out. I found group working interesting but distracting, as I paid intense attention to the group dynamic instead of the task set. I did not learn in these environments. I felt keenly in group situations when one voice became too dominant at the cost of others. We were expected to collaborate without having any nuanced understanding as to how it works. What successful collaboration looks like versus when it goes wrong. What would often happen with working in groups was that one clever, dominant student took over and the rest of us checked out, becoming passive learners – when the whole point was for it to be a collaborative learning experience.

- **Processing time.** To do well at something, I needed time to map and process the information.

- **To pay attention.** I had (and continue to have) a rich imagination and internal learning world, and so to really engage with something, I needed to shut down from the real world slightly. I tried to develop my own mechanisms for this. I would look down at the paper and doodle when listening, but the teacher often thought this meant I was not listening. Often, I had to sit next to the teacher because they wanted to ensure I was engaging. Ironically, I would then make sure I looked like I was engaging, and that meant I was not really taking in the information. I was very well behaved and loved learning, but all school reports read,

'Hannah would do well if she paid attention.'

- **A clear objective.** I needed to know what the point of the learning was, why we were doing it. If I knew that I excelled. If I did not know that I was disengaged. Often the reason why we were doing something was withheld – the answer being 'Just do it.' But why?
- **Time away.** I often got severe tonsillitis and was off unwell, which I think was the result of my body absorbing the stress of the experience of school. Later, in sixth form, I often self-soothed by staying home. This understandably annoyed teachers, and my attendance records were terrible. But I needed, vitally, this downtime.

What I did not benefit from

- **The constant company of large groups of people.** I got absolutely exhausted through the simple fact of being in a large class group all day. Too much time in the company of other people.
- **Predicted poor school grades.** I was expected to achieve incredibly low GCSE and A-level grades, but I got high grades. This really made me realize how much the teachers and I were misunderstanding what engagement looked like.
- **Negative comments.** I would crucify myself over negative comments made by a teacher or fellow student. In my teen years, I was paralysed by the awareness that others were judging my physical appearance and commenting within earshot. Teenage boys continually remarking on my breasts. Group toxic-girl culture. Best friends sleeping with boyfriends, then calling to laugh about it. Friends persuading you to cut your hair, then laughing at you for having short hair. Forcing you to weigh yourself in front of

them, examining parts of your body and criticizing them. None of this was kept under control by the school.

- **Competition.** I found competition uninteresting and unmotivating, meaning I often came last or somewhere near the bottom.

I was sensitive to

- **Vulnerable members of the class.** I was very aware who was struggling and why. At my school there were a lot of kids who were very damaged by their life experiences. I would go to great lengths to try to help, but didn't know what I was doing, so I'd get overwhelmed and exhausted.
- **Sensory experience.** I struggled with the strip neon lights, which gave me migraines. The itchy uniform, which gave me eczema. The level of volume in the class often left me disorientated, and I would zone out. I would fall into deep sleep after school, exhausted, damaging my night-time sleep rhythms.
- **Strong emotions.** I was strongly moved by things we were shown in our learning; sometimes I was moved through joy, sometimes through sorrow. I would try to sit at the back of everything so that no one could see me crying. I learned how to cry without making any noise, how to cover up emotion.

I have constructed that list not because my experience was interesting or unusual, but because it is common. I looked at the system of success in schools, observed who did well and why, looked at myself in comparison and thought, 'I am not those things; therefore, I am not of value, I am a failure, I am a problem.' The thing is, I did have a standout skill: my sensitivity. It is my best asset; it is what I am good at. But there was no measurement system for it. Two of my siblings are very dyslexic, to the point that they struggle to read or write at all, and a lot of the students I work with for many reasons sit outside the mainstream education system. They too have this understanding of themselves as someone who does not fit, who is not of value – it eats away at their confidence, it shapes the path they take, it saps their mental health. I live in the town I grew up in, and I still flinch when I see the now grown-up kids who did fit. I see them and think, 'They think I am a loser; they are winners.' Amazing how binary a subconscious can be. Because obviously it's much more complex than that. Those individuals simply fitted that system of measurement we were in. I did not. We both have value, and it's different. But my ego sometimes struggles with that.

We have a big problem with othering narratives that do not fit the main. We hide those narratives. To hear them destabilizes the system. They are often even considered a threat. I could endlessly list examples of this. I offer you a short one. I was working with a group of pupils at risk of exclusion in a big comprehensive in an area with socioeconomic challenges but within a rich town – lots of inequality. I worked with a filmmaker, someone I have collaborated with previously and with whom I have established a good working practice. Our approach, open to change, is that we get to know the pupils, figure out what their concerns are, observe the type of behaviour they are showing us, notice how they respond to each other, and we base the project around that. In this instance, the pupils were massively misbehaving – I mean, imagine the worst and triple it. It took us three sessions to get them to sit down and do a single activity. The volume of noise in the room was funny. They were wild cards, twenty wild cards all in one room.

For a long time, they resented our presence, were openly

hostile. But once they started talking to us, they told us that they did not all know each other very well, they were from different classes and year groups, it was a big school, they knew each other by reputation, they had heard of things the others had done. They joked that they had been showing off for each other, walking up to meet their reputation. Bravado. Once they put that down, they began an amazingly involved conversation about being on the verge of exclusion; they started giving each other advice, being incredibly sensitive to one another, showing real empathy. With, of course, occasional outrageous behaviours.

The filmmaker and I looked at each other and knew they had led us to where the project needed to focus. We made the focus 'at risk of exclusion'. The students were given to believe that if they took part in the project, worked hard on the film, it would be shown to the whole school and at a local film festival. They made the film, they interviewed the head teacher about how it feels to manage exclusions, they talked to the teachers they had reported to, they shared their life stories. It was a bumpy ride, but they did it. And they didn't just do it, they cooperated, they showed such care for one another, young lads sitting listening to each other, saying, 'Yes, me too.' The film was bloody beautiful, them saying things like, 'I know it feels like you can't do it and you are on your own, that you have walked up and lost too many chances, but maybe you have not had the right conditions, maybe be kind to yourself, you can do it, learn to walk the line, you will be so proud of yourself.' We were so proud of them. They had made something greater than the sum of their parts, greater than the promise of their behaviour, they had connected and committed and shared.

I heard that the school had seen the finished film and though they had been happy in abstract to commit to the theme of it, they were not happy putting out a film that mentioned that they had some students at risk of exclusion, even though the film had a positive message. It was felt that it put the school in a bad light, it was not the story they wanted to tell, it did not fit with their values. The film was not shown internally or at the film festival. I have been haunted by the significance of that occurrence. I don't know if the students gave it another thought, but it felt like a betrayal of their reality, a silencing. Interestingly, a lot of the young people displayed signs of being highly sensitive. And I know that a lot of them grew up in difficult environments. We are ignoring proportions that do not fit. It ruins the story that education is fit for purpose, that it is successful.

As explored earlier in this chapter, it not unusual to experience not fitting into a system and think, 'It's me that is the problem, the system must be right, because the system is bigger than me. Someone designed it like that, and it must be like that for a good reason.' But sometimes systems are wrong or, if not wrong, then in a process of complicated change.

***

Now, I want us to return to thinking about our educational leaders, our teachers. What skills and traits are prevalent in teaching staff? Research has shown that HSPs are strongly drawn to professions such as teaching – where care and clear meaning are key components of the role. Lord Knight said at the end of his interview: 'A good teacher sees the attributes of each member their class.' So, what skill is useful in understanding and seeing the attributes of a class? You guessed it! Sensitivity is a phenomenally useful trait and skill for teaching. An article on Teachstone (an online resource for educational staff) by Mamie Morrow asks the question, why is teacher sensitivity important? 'Research tells us that teachers who are aware of and respond to each child supportively facilitate the ability of all children in the classroom to explore actively and learn.' So teachers using the skill of sensitivity are more likely to carry the whole class with them in their diversity. That's good, isn't it? Sensitivity means you are more likely to have really considered how to carry the whole class on the journey that they need to take.

For many children, teachers are their first experience of leadership outside the home. Their first exposure to hierarchy, to the values of how the world works. So it is fantastic that we have lots of highly sensitive teachers, because that means pupils get to see what sensitivity looks like in leadership. Teacher sensitivity is useful in the current education system – it sort of bridges where the system fails. Teachers are often highly empathic, good information-processors, emotionally intelligent and conscientious. Not always, but often. So how does the system treat that skill and trait of teacher sensitivity?

I would like to introduce you to Gemma. We first met in 2019. She got in touch following a thought piece I had done on the radio, and we had arranged to talk about sensitivity and education. I called at the appointed time and she said, 'Funny you should call right at this moment, because right this very second I am standing outside the head teacher's office, about to go in and hand in my resignation. Partly after listening to your programme.'

It was an important moment for her, so we ended the call. And in the following months, I thought of her often, wondering if she had left her job and worrying if I was partly responsible. I really hoped she felt she had made the right decision. We made an appointment to speak again.

Gemma: My name is Gemma, and I used to be a teacher, head of department.

Hannah: Gemma, can I ask, how do you feel about having left your teaching job? Did you leave?

Gemma: Yes, I did leave. I was a head of department in a secondary school. I had been a teacher for quite a few years, really loved it, but there were just a few things that were making me re-evaluate it. I was thinking, 'Am I in the right job, am I doing the right thing?', and those doubts sort of become a little bit overwhelming. Then I listened to what you said on Radio 4, and I thought, 'Yeah, maybe I do need to take the plunge and be confident and do it', and then just sort of re-evaluate where I was. So yeah, it was strange when you rang, because I was literally just about to hand over the letter to resign.

Hannah: How do you feel about that decision now?

Gemma: I'm much less stressed. I miss the children and I miss talking about history, that is a big loss to me. But mentally and physically I am so much healthier now that I've given that up. It's given me time to re-evaluate and realize that I was good at my job.

Hannah: What was it about being sensitive that you felt that the school environment wasn't particularly catering towards?

Gemma: I think you must be a sensitive person to be a good teacher. And I was a good teacher, and the school was great – it's the profession that does not value sensitivity. I was overworking to try and make sure that my students' needs were met, because I was very sensitive to wanting them to succeed.

I wanted to be good at my job so that they did well, and I was just working too many hours to try and make sure that happened. I was exhausted. And I just thought, 'I'm now detrimental to my students because I'm so tired.' I was being that stereotypical, overly sensitive person. I was crying a lot. I was taking everything badly.

Hannah: And is that something that you heard other teachers say about the education system? Do you know anyone else who felt that way?

Gemma: Yeah, I can't think of a single ex-colleague who doesn't feel that way. But a lot of them are not in the fortunate position I was. I could leave, and I did. They all say the same thing, that if you are a good teacher, you are conscientious, and that means being completely worn down by paperwork and constant criticism for something that you are working hard for. I think a lot of my colleagues who were good at their job were very sensitive people, and I think that's why they were good, and it's such a shame that a lot of us are leaving.

Hannah: I'm really interested in whether you feel the education system caters to sensitivity as a valuable trait in young people within the school environment.

Gemma: I was a humanities teacher, so we were always trying to encourage creativity. It's one of the higher-order thinking skills. But I didn't think that the exams valued that criterion. There was much, much more emphasis put on maths and literacy. There were a lot of things closing, like they were closing music lessons, and there was less time spent on the arts. The attitude was that creativity was a waste of time – why do that when you could be training them to pass exams?

[I am going to intervene here with something Sir Ken Robinson said in his talk 'Schools Kill Creativity,' which is that creativity is the skill needed for innovation. That children are willing to be wrong, willing to have a go at getting an answer to something, and that school is a system of learning to get the answer right rather than being willing to take a chance on possibly being wrong. As a result, by the time they are adults, they have lost that capacity, it has been educated out of them, which means the real resource of our ability to innovate is educated out of us. While schools have shown a growing trend of interest in the willingness to be wrong and have started to appreciate that mistake-making is of value, this is only if it does not get in the way of exam grades.]

Gemma: To get them to jump through hoops like that was hard for me. One of the reasons that I couldn't carry on. You just must get them through the system. The attitude is, 'Well, that is how the world works, right?' But what about their wellbeing? The job of a teacher now is to follow a curriculum that is dictated to you not by the school, but by the government. And what I was seeing was that highly intelligent, creative children were being forced down a system, and that felt sad to me.

Hannah: What does your job entail now?

Gemma: I am a fundraiser for a very ethical company. It really fits all my values, and my sensitivity is championed instead of being pushed aside. I get to help meet people's needs, get people the support they deserve. And having made the shift out of teaching, it's nice to have my sensitivity valued and praised for once. My colleagues, you can tell that they're all passionate people, and they are sensitive, and that's nice. I feel like it's a much more positive aspect to my personality than it used to be.

Hannah: I'm trying to ask how society could change a bit to make better use of the characteristic of sensitivity? What change would you like to see?

Gemma: I would like to see sensitivity being understood in all its different guises rather than just seen as, if you're sensitive, you're easily offended, or you're easily upset, because while those are traits I do have, I'm also hypersensitive to other people's needs or situations, which is what made me a good teacher. And I just don't think anybody says that. That being a sensitive person, and being sensitive to what's going on around you, is a massively positive thing. So, instead of people saying, you know, 'Stop being sensitive, get over it,' I think people should be saying, 'It's really good that you have this type of sensitivity that is a positive attribute.' So, I think if sensitivity was discussed in different ways, rather than just as being sensitive and being sad about things, there are some positive aspects to it, and I think that's what we need to see change.

I loved talking to Gemma and was reassured to know that she was glad she had changed her job. Speaking to her I became fascinated with this contradictory tension at the centre of education – the devaluing of pupil sensitivity, but the reliance on teacher sensitivity. How contradictory, exploitative, disorientating.

Sensitivity is what drew Gemma to teaching. Her understanding and care for the needs of her pupils. But the overemphasis on testing, and her conscientiousness, had caused her to overwork, resulting in what she felt was 'bad sensitive'. Initially I thought surely there is no such thing as bad sensitive. But I have come to realize Gemma is right – when a system we are trying to exist in is not working for us, and we are writhing under its conditions, that is bad sensitive. I wonder how common Gemma's experience is within teaching staff.

It's interesting to me that there is such a problem with staff retention within education. Statistics published by the DfE state that, of teachers who qualified in 2014, just 67.4 per cent were still in service after a period of five years, in 2019. I cannot help but feel that the system not only mines children for one dominant resource, but that it ironically mines the resources and skill of sensitivity from its teaching staff. As far as I know, teachers don't get paid more for being empathic to their students, they get paid more if they repeatedly get their pupils to pass exams to a sufficient standard.

Something important has struck me while writing this chapter that had not occurred to me previously – sensitivity is political, or rather it is politick. When one discusses sensitivity, it always begins with the individual not fitting the system. But the diversity of us is not something new, and these discussions have made me realize how common this not fitting is, in so many forms of intelligence and skill. Lord Knight was right to compare what we have done ecologically to the soil in over-farming commodities with the over-mining of human commodities, skills and traits. We have this vast range of us. Just think through all the people you know, and the diversity of their traits and skills. What a wealth. What potential. I wonder, are we wasting resources through a short-sighted need to keep things the same? Sometimes it is indeed the individual who needs to learn to fit the system. But sometimes, the system has forgotten how to change.

Something that has been gestured at in this chapter's interviews is the relationship between the humanities, the arts and empathic citizens. American philosopher Martha C Nussbaum makes the case, in her book *Not for Profit*, that education has lost focus of its aims and intentions. She argues that education is now treated as if its sole function is to serve the economy. The skills of critical thinking, philosophy and empathy are significantly deprioritized. This is indeed short-sighted. We are losing our ability to criticize authority and to deal with complex global challenges. Her book argues that the loss of these skills places the health of the world under significant threat. These skills are vital to us all. But this is not evident in our education system.

The thing I find funny about this is that we have whole glorious swathes of people who are brilliant at challenging authority, and others who have extraordinary sympathy and skill to work with and support the marginalized and different. We are a question-asking species, it is innate, we have the skills in us we need in order to be capable and competent to deal with complex global problems. But we have to stop educating these abilities out of people. We have to stop deprioritizing these skills. It is essential that we broaden our education system, learn to reward, and contain, stories broader than those that are directly and obviously economically productive.

Gemma described the humanities as requiring 'higher-order thinking' skills. In terms of the relationship between sensitivity and creativity, this has long been anecdotal within many cultures. Psychologists David Bridges and Haline E Schendan conducted a piece of research into individual differences and creativity, and in 2019 wrote a paper called 'Sensitive Individuals Are More Creative'. Their findings showed that sensitive, open people are more creative due to 'a complex interplay of multiple traits and their associated biological pathways', with particular reference to certain genetic interactions and the development of their neurotransmitter systems.

As Sir Ken Robinson argues, insights happen when we make new or unexpected connections, and divergent thinking is an essential capacity for creativity, or an opportunity to ask powerful questions about issues. Our young people are abundant in creativity in all its diversity, they are not afraid to take a chance, to innovate. But we systematically educate this out of them and give them instead a fear of getting the answer wrong through repeated testing.

Creativity is an extraordinary resource, incredibly valuable for a changing society. In 1968, distinguished scientist George Land, with Beth Jarman, conducted a research study to test the creativity of 1,600 children ranging in age from three to five years, asking them to look at a problem and come up with different and innovative ways of solving it. Dr Land had devised a similar test for NASA to help select innovative engineers and scientists. He later tested the same children at ten years of age, and again at fifteen.

The results were astounding. The proportion of people who scored at the 'Genius Level' were:

- among five-year-olds: 98 per cent
- among ten-year-olds: 30 per cent
- among fifteen-year-olds: 12 per cent
- same test given to 280,000 adults (average age of thirty-one): 2 per cent

CREATIVITY SCORES AT GENIUS LEVEL

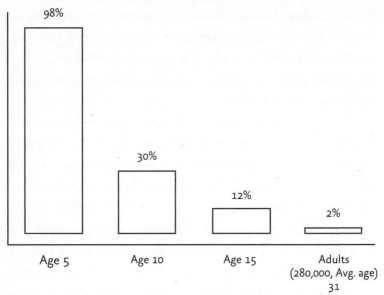

According to Land, the primary reason for this is that there are two types of thinking processes when it comes to creativity:

- **Convergent thinking:** where you judge ideas, criticize them, refine them, combine them and improve them, all of which happens in your conscious thought.
- **Divergent thinking:** where you imagine new ideas, original ones, which are different from what has come before but which may be rough to start with. This often happens subconsciously.

Land notes that, throughout school, we are teaching children to try and use both kinds of thinking at the same time, which is impossible. Competing neurons in the brain will be fighting each other, and it is as if your mind is having a shouting match with itself. Land suggests that, if you want your child to retain their ability to be creative, encourage them to let their mind run free while they come up with ideas, and only afterwards evaluate them.

I think that the education system does not provide favourable conditions for innovation. The current trend for embracing learning from mistakes is mere lip service, and individual achievement and exam-taking ultimately reign high above all other types of intelligence.

It has been said that each educational system is a mirror that reflects the culture. So, what is our culture, what are our systems creating? And do we have the luxury of keeping them as they are? In *The Highly Sensitive Person*, Elaine Aron wonders whether we ask enough spiritual, moral and philosophical questions: 'They are always being answered, implicitly, by a society's values and behaviours – whom it respects, whom it loves, whom it fears, who it leaves to languish unhoused and unfed.' Our moral values, our philosophical questions live in who we hear, who we silence, the systems we implement, our relationship to the movement of change. We benefit from diversity in all its forms. We are an ecosystem of intelligences and traits and skills. At the moment we have a monopolized idea about who and what have value. What are the implications of those values? If we follow down the line, using the values of competition, individual testing, productivity and economic success – where do we end up collectively? Are we providing an appropriate response?

To close this chapter, on my favourite subject, I want to offer you a poem by one of my favourite poets, Salena Godden:

Before you jump

Before you go to the doctors
and take their anti-depressants
and before you sign up for a shrink
or some counselling for your
escalating anxiety and panic attacks
and before you give yourself
yet another scolding
for feeling overtired all the time
for cancelling things
for feeling hypersensitive
for not going faster and
for going quicker
and for not being more decisive
please check you're not in fact in mourning
living in a world ruled by rude twats
impatient and selfish arseholes
in a calamity of chaos and panic
in a careless and noisy world
governed by reckless bastards
that should listen to the nightmares
of the children of the future.

5. Sensitive challenges

I couldn't write this book without devoting a chapter to exploring some of the challenges of being highly sensitive. There are many reported challenges, among them:

- Feeling things strongly and being easily hurt emotionally
- Being easily startled or overwhelmed
- Sleeping poorly
- Feeling uncomfortable in loud or overstimulating places for long periods
- Engaging in and being affected by the problems of others
- Having difficulty letting go
- Struggling with boundaries
- Not always being heard
- All this often leading to compromised mental health.

There is so very much to say on this aspect of sensitivity that I cannot cover each challenge in depth. I am going to focus predominantly on the experience of 'overwhelm', because overwhelm can be the conclusion of taking in a whole range of sensory and emotional variables.

Highly sensitive people are notably prone to overwhelm.

Overwhelm is an emotional state where you are struggling to cope with the variables of your current situation. It all gets too much. I think of it as being like a piece of machinery overheating and stopping working properly. I am learning to notice early when these days are coming, and I have given them a name – overdraft days. Because it is metaphorically like a bank account that has gone into the red. Or like a laptop overheating or that bit of a plug where the wires meet the cable without covering, like your soul is wedged up in your throat sideways, like a too-full water jug on a wonky picnic table, like too many instructions coming into a router, like a sky full of planes and an air-traffic controller who speaks a different language.

On an overdraft day your senses are jangled, and on these days, in a very literal and physical way, your nervous system and senses protest. In my experience, sensitive overwhelm is a total lack of capacity, having reached the end of what I can offer, being unable to accept any further data or information from others' emotional needs or logistical arrangements. Once in that state it is hard to find contingency or capacity of mind to do anything other than the instincts the animal brain and body systems are asking for – isolation. For me, that means a period of shutting up shop, fusing out.

A lot of my identity is tied up in being good with people, in helping people, in being very sociable, so these days do not sit entirely easy with me; it has taken a long time not to self-shame about the need to retreat. And it is not always taken well: I have friends and family members who do not understand, and that is OK, because I know it is what I need. Overwhelm days are incapacitating, a sign of a system rebelling against itself, a life built around everything but sensitivity. I think these overwhelm days are the biggest part of the story that we tell ourselves about there being something wrong with us. Because it means not always being able to make the same decisions that others can.

In 2010 in London, I was at a house party of some close friends from university. They had a lot of parties. I knew most people there; it was loud and full on, and I was happy to see everyone. I got into a conversation with a friend, let's call him John. John said to me, 'Why do you not live in London with the rest of us? It's great! So much to do, it would be so great for your writing, and you would be near us all. Stop being a baby and just move to live near us all.'

I answered with something like, 'Yeah, I would love to, but I get easily overwhelmed, I need a lot of downtime, I need to connect with people more one on one. When I am in London, I am very aware of the facial expressions of everyone on the tube and I'm affected by how they might be feeling, I start to worry about people, it feels a lot to move through. When I am in London I tend to oversubscribe and overcommit myself and find there is no downtime, only time overpeopled, overtalked, sensory overload. I like walking down the street and having space around me, hearing the birds, the woman on the silversmith stall saying hi, I need to be alone and feel my aloneness.'

'Well, that's a shame,' John said. 'The trick is to block it all out, ignore other people, don't worry about them, push through the crowd, make your own space.'

I went to get a drink and while pouring myself one thought, yes, I imagine he is right, I am being silly, I don't need any of the things I think I do, I just need to learn to block out people and places, then I can be with my friends.

I applied for several jobs in London, but each time I went for an interview or flat-hunting, I would come back and fuse out, falling completely asleep on the train, the sitting-room floor, at my desk at work. I was left feeling so wiped out that no matter how tempting the job, I could not bring myself to say yes. And yet I still so wanted to be with all my friends, I missed the belonging.

I have thought long and hard about that fleeting conversation in subsequent years, whether it is a choice to be so engaged with one's environment and surrounding people, whether I could just learn to stop getting overwhelmed. But I am configured the way I am and, instead of fighting that, I made a different kind of life for myself in Norwich, a smallish city in the east of England, working for an arts organization, walking in every day via the market and saying hello to the woman on the silversmith stall. I would take myself on long walks around the city at night, up and down the rows of Victorian terraced houses, looking in at other people's sitting rooms, smelling other people's suppers cooking, noticing the light slowly tipping out of the day. When possible I would take myself to the beach on weekends and walk a long way, following the edge of the sea and the sand. I developed important one-to-one friendships, fell in love a few times, began to write. I had space to manage myself, I had space to notice when I was close to being overwhelmed. I was in an environment that offered the right kind of conditions. I had learned how to supply myself with the right conditions, even though they were at the cost of leaving behind a big group of friends.

Overwhelm shows up differently for everyone, but for me the signs are: being easily startled, falling asleep without warning, negative self-talk, circular thinking about slights, a strong feeling of needing to retreat from the world. High sensitivity overlaps with autism in that it shares environmental sensitivities such as strong awareness of touch and sound. It is different from autism in terms of interpersonal nuances. For me this strong sense of environmental factors is mainly visual. The aesthetics of a room sometimes can be noisy, as if it is shouting that it is not in harmony with itself: it's incredibly inconvenient for a swell of this to happen at other people's houses, and I have in the past rearranged hotel rooms. I also think extensively about what other people think and feel, which can use up quite a lot of brain space. Therefore, I need a lot of downtime, on my own, time to digest and process. And that is true of all HSPs. HSPs have a lot of information coming in all the time, because that is how they are constructed.

To be a successful HSP thriving in the world, it is important to find ways to manage yourself well. And that is going to be different for everyone. I, for example, struggle with migraines and poor sleep and low self-worth. I repeatedly try and mitigate against these outcomes. I know that what works for me is significant alone time and regular yoga to shift my breathing pattern. However, sometimes self-intervention is easier said than done – overwhelm feels chaotic, like a whirlpool with no pattern. It can feel like it is something swirling out and away from you with you inside it. But it does follow a pattern. And if we can figure out what a pattern is, we can learn how to intervene. Here is my pattern, for example:

- Overworking or a very long continuous period in others' company with no alone time
- Start to feel panicked and stressed, grow more sensitive
- Start to pay more attention to negative things people say and do, interpret them as being personal
- Start to stew on the injustice of some situation or other, think it is my fault
- Feel overwhelmed and distressed, feel that the house is messy, that I need to get more organized, make a list, tidy up, try

and achieve huge pieces of work but do not have enough capacity, get exhausted
- Negative self-talk begins – why can't I just not be tired?
- Start to feel other people are too much, feel strong need to retreat from others
- Ignore that need, carry on
- End up completely overwhelmed, unable to connect or engage with others
- Take a few days to regain stasis.

Obviously, that is an unhelpful cycle. And many HSPs will have something along those lines. Learning what your early warning signs are, knowing what your pattern is, is important, so that you can intervene, avoid reaching total overwhelm. I have noticed that my signs include:

- Wanting to leave rooms
- Feeling unsettled and unsure why
- Increasingly avoiding eye contact
- Wanting to nap
- Feeling sudden sweeping empathic urges for others when they are not near to me
- Overworrying about what I am wearing
- Turning over and over perceived negative comments.

HSP brains are always doing an extra layer of activity: to feel comfortable and safe, they need a lot of information. They are so tuned in to others' tone, feelings and actions that it's incredibly easy for the skill of empathy to become a problem if they don't have clear boundaries in place. It's important for HSPs to reground themselves separately from others, to take time apart to settle.

If nothing else, their nervous system needs to reset.

I would like to introduce you to someone highly articulate in the skills that the highly sensitive need in order to thrive.

———————————

Barbara: My name is Barbara Allen. I am director, senior mentor, speaker and trainer at Growing Unlimited Consultancy. I am also the founder of the National Centre for High Sensitivity and was director there from 2010 to 2019.

Hannah: You work a lot helping highly sensitive people to live successful lives, helping them with strategies for dealing with overwhelm and so forth. If you had to say something to the world out there about HSPs, what would it be?

Barbara: If I was to talk to the world out there, I would say don't worry about HSPs. Try not to get in their way, because that's what's happening and that's what is sad. HSPs get a bad name because there are a lot of people out there looking at HSPs only when they are having a hard day, giving a broken picture of HSPs, and that makes me angry because if people stopped saying no to HSPs all the time, we would have a lot less broken HSPs.

Hannah: You produced a set of videos to help parents of highly sensitive teenagers. Can you tell me about that?

Barbara: Yes, they are aimed at people who are doing an internet search because they are despairing as to what to do with their highly sensitive teenager.

HS teenagers experience a lot of overwhelm. They are often

deep thinkers, they process deeply, and that takes time. And HSPs look at things from a variety of perspectives, and that can be challenging in a school environment, for example, because let's say the teacher has been talking about something and the class are responding to it, a highly sensitive child or teenager will take longer to digest this information, assessing it, considering it, so if they want to add something to the discussion, it is most likely that the teacher has moved on to another topic before they are ready to contribute. HS teenagers often arrive at 'aha' moments before others; also, often HSP teenagers have the experience, when in a mixed trait group, of coming up with a topic, saying here is my little bit of wisdom or thought. And then the conversation moves on, and three hours later, the group arrive at that same conclusion. They can easily feel devalued and not heard.

Hannah: What do you think is happening when someone reaches overwhelm?

Barbara: Taking in too much information, literally. HSPs are long-term thinkers. It can read as daydreaming or zoning out, but it's processing, entering their mind to work something out. And I think we should leave them to it, to do all the thinking and processing that they need, then they can share in whatever way they feel is right.

Hannah: What do HSPs need in order to thrive?

Barbara: Flexibility. School is a system of command and obedience, not flexibility. It's not saying what is needed here and innovating. School is about saying we need you to do the following, so do the following and life is expected to be an extension of that. You can understand that if you have 70 per cent of the population whose minds are a certain way and have certain needs, then the people designing the education system are going to build it in the image of the majority, and it is most likely designed by people with the traits of that 70 per cent.

The thing is to recognize that people are like plants and they have different places in the garden where they should be. So, an HS child, if you don't find out exactly who they are, they are going to really suffer, because they are different, they don't fit those systems, and not fitting a system is overwhelming.

The big problem facing HSPs now is that we have a culture where HSPs are taught to behave differently to their natural way of being. So, what you have is, instead of an 70/30 per cent bias, you have a 95 per cent/5 per cent bias. HS people try to pretend to be something that they are not. And as we all know, if you change something in nature, like you remove the wolves and the wild and things like that, it challenges the survival of that environment.

Hannah: I'm curious. My main experience being a highly sensitive person is just being so worried about other people. So worried, and so aware of reading what they're feeling. And the answer to that from the world seems to be, well, if that is challenging for you then just don't worry about anyone else, stop taking the information in; but it does not feel as simple as that.

Barbara: No, it is not as simple as that, it is how HSPs are made. Your philosophy of life, I think, is 'We all need to make it.' And so being hyperaware of others and how they are feeling, your brain is looking all the time for subtleties, complexities, patterns – mirror neurons firing off left, right and centre – it creates strong emotions. And it's our emotions that prompt action. And so if emotions are more intense, because of all the extra firing of the mirror neurons, we are prompted to act. This then merges with your philosophy, which is – we all have to make it. When innate empathy collides with a belief system, to provoke action.

Trouble is, to consistently have high empathy, you can spend your whole time thinking, what is wrong with me? Should I just stop thinking like this? Reading all the time that others are suffering and need help is kind of exhausting and it can reach a point of saturation.

Hannah: Do you think that the propensity to become overwhelmed means that it thwarts HSPs' possibilities for life success?

Barbara: There are HSPs everywhere who are successful, who don't even know they're sensitive, but they've had just enough of the right environment. And they also have freedom and flexibility in their lives. Partly by choosing the right friends and partner, and partly by choosing the right workspace and career to be able to be the best that they can be. And they often outdo everybody. They only start to suffer if their circumstances create a very unhelpful environment. HSPs I meet who have not had their environment significantly get in their way are often leading-edge thinkers.

Hannah: What do you feel is the function of the highly sensitive?

Barbara: The role of HSPs is to bring everything together, like the filaments of a network. We perceive where the filaments meet and join. We understand connections and the things between things. HSPs perceive. HSPs are often in the background somewhere, being consulted as to their perceptions. HSPs are subtle and complex. They understand nuance.

We are now living in a power structure that is based on one way of thinking – bigger, better, more. And as a result, there is a lack of respect for alternative traits. For example, a lack of respect for long-term planning, sharing, mutual support. Anything that is given value in our society is about how much money you get for it.

That is something HSPs really struggle with. They struggle with doing anything that they do not find meaningful. Trouble is, a lot of the jobs HSPs are drawn to are not well paid, and so that is not good, it feels for them like a lack of respect for their skillset. They are drawn to those jobs because they are drawn to committing their lives to meaning.

In the past, there were all sorts of things and traits valued that did not produce, but were essential to keeping a society glued together in a different kind of way. It's innate in sensitive people, that ability to see the bigger picture, an awareness that there are communities and environments out there bigger than you and that we are connected. And different HSPs will explore that in different ways: through their work, spiritually, chemically, on a molecular level. Often the meaning of something is so obvious to HSPs, and other people struggle to see it. Their brains are fast, very quick connections are made in things that others may not necessarily see.

Hannah: Trouble is, we live in a culture whereby if one was to say, 'I know this is going to happen,' the culture would say, 'Show me how you know, we need the workings, the facts.'

Barbara: They're asking you for the mechanics of how you got there. They're saying, if I don't understand the mechanics, then I don't believe how you've got there. So therefore, you didn't get there. Which is not logical. If you arrive at a place in the desert, and someone says, I don't know how you got here so you're not here, that is ridiculous, because clearly, I am here, physically present.

There was a study conducted on the brain to do with the aha moment. And the findings are that the aha moment is so fast, that it is very hard to time. I think a lot of sensitive people have this experience where they know things and they don't know why. And a lot of people interpret that as spiritual, but it's connecting things, deep-storing information and interpreting, arriving at aha moments often, original thought – it happens in less than a second.

Hannah: Yes, I have had moments of knowing something and not understanding how I knew it – like a flash of insight. My partner and I have been together for ten years and in that time we have moved house a lot. We don't argue much, but something that used to always cause friction was house-hunting. We would go into a house, and I would know straight away if it was somewhere we could live. I just knew. And he would say, but how can you know, show me the facts. Sometimes I couldn't even find words for it, it was a feeling. And so sometimes, being unable to prove that it was not the right house, I conceded and said OK, yes, let's go with that house, and sure enough after a few months some problem emerged – a cruel landlord, a leaking shower, excessively loud neighbours, mould. And after four years of this type of house-related mini-disaster happening, he said to me, OK next time we must house-hunt, whatever skill it is that you are using to do that knowing seems to be correct, so I will trust it. And I cannot tell you how much that meant to me. It was like he had said he trusted my instincts, my method. And that felt huge.

Barbara: That is a great example of two different types working together. And what that means is you give the other the mandate for what their skills are, an authority to do what they are good at. That is two sides working together.

If there was a war on or something, there might have been a role for the HSP-type brain and a role for the other types. For example, there might be a war that had started, and nobody could stop it. There would be certain mandates that you would give to these two parts, so that you could work together to make use of the best that you've got. You can't act like each other; you must have different traits and skills to get the best outcome. And that is what your partner was doing: he gave you his trust, he trusts your skillset.

Hannah: Yes, it is one of the reasons I love him, he considers us to be equal.

I would like to ask you about emotional mirroring. What do you think emotional mirroring is for? [Emotional mirroring is where you re-create the feeling and emotions of the person that you are around in yourself. Highly sensitive people do this a lot.]

Barbara: Emotional mirroring, its function – so that we don't explode everything. When your mirror neurons fire, they create a sensation in you that you know how the other person is feeling. And that then makes you respond appropriately. If you don't do that, you will respond inappropriately, and all responses in all animals are about survival. So, if you do not recognize when something needs your help or support, for instance, if a baby's crying and you are not able to know how painful that is, you won't respond to sort out the need in the child. Failing to respond to the needs of yourself or another is serious, it's serious for the survival of the species. Mirror neurons make us respond, make us act. Every emotion and every response are designed for the survival of the species.

Hannah: And my final question – you mentioned that you identify as being highly sensitive. I am curious as to how you manage this in relation to your clearly very successful work. I mean, I imagine you spend a lot of time with people in distress, your empathy must get tired.

Barbara: I am aware of the propensity for overwhelm. I work for myself deliberately so that I have control over my working environment. I am boundaried about what I will and will not do. I have learned to speak up when something is not working for me. I allow myself a lot of rest time, even if that means resting on the sofa and watching something on my iPad and I have learned not to feel guilty about that. I am picky about who I collaborate with and clients I take on. I only work with people with open minds, people who are capable of compassion not just to client groups, but to their colleagues as well, and who are not so interested in promoting themselves that they would do that to the detriment of the whole project. So, I am very, very careful.

Hannah: Funny what you say about resting and not feeling guilty. In my office I have a big bean bag and sometimes after writing for a few hours my brain feels fried and I feel the pull of wanting a power nap, but I do feel guilty about it.

In terms of collaborators, I too have had to start being incredibly careful as to the values of the people I work closely with. I have had experiences where it has been devastating when someone's real values have been revealed and I discover that their circle of self-care does not extend to anyone but themselves. I get very upset in those situations. It is those situations that often trigger overwhelm days for me.

Barbara: Yes, I really understand this. When one rubs up against them it can feel almost dangerous, because there is such misunderstanding of values. I think at the start of a project it can be hard to tell if someone shares the same values as you and if you are both excited about the project. My advice is to hold back, observe them, notice if they take energy.

HSPs usually have quite a high level of self-doubt, they ask themselves a lot of questions. It's quite a different energy from how we run highly powered companies, for example. But I think a successful model of HSPs being in the world looks like having HSPs and non-HSPs around you. For example, my husband is a non-HSP. And one of the things that at first made me angry but now I value, is after a long day I will tell him lots of realizations and the intricacies of things. Often he will respond with yes, that's interesting. And I will think, hmmm, I was expecting more engagement, so I will dig down deeper. It used to really annoy me that he would not move to meet the depth of the conversation. But now I really value it. Now I realize, oh, I don't always need go down and inwards in thinking like that, it would be exhausting to always be depth-charging.

I think being in a relationship with a non-HSP can prevent us from spiralling into such a depth of thinking. Sometimes, we find it hard to climb out and we get exhausted by our own thinking. I think it's very valuable to also be around non-HSPs, to have conversations where we surface.

Hannah: I really appreciate your time and your brain and you and your sharing of your practice and life.

Barbara: And thank you, because, you know, I don't have conversations like this that often. You've been part of my self-care today.

It was really interesting to talk with someone whose job it is to help HSPs struggling with their sensitivity. There is a lot to be gleaned from speaking with Barbara Allen, but I was particularly taken by the fact that she mentioned the education system and its inflexibility – flexibility being one of the most helpful things for struggling HSPs. I was also struck by the statistics of how many HSPs try to change themselves, or rather hide. To pretend to be something you are not is exhausting, full-time work that is often unsuccessful and leads to much misunderstanding. And the implications of that are further reaching than those that impact solely on the individual. As Barbara Allen says, 'If you change something in nature, it challenges survival of that environment.'

There is such stigma attached to sensitivity that many HSPs do wish to be like others; they are taught, or learn, to be different to their nature. And that might work for some, but for others not. And as Barbara Allen also says, 'Not fitting a system is overwhelming.'

Barbara Allen offered me a new perspective. HSPs are consistently told by systems that they are wrong for not fitting. But HSPs need to zone out, to fuse down – it is part of how they are built. The idea of trusting HSPs when they are doing that seems simple, but in fact is radical. Don't interfere. Let them get on with it. Seems counterintuitive when someone is clearly doing something different. But yes, trust them, allow them that contingency around how they engage and process.

I love Barbara Allen's equal emphasis on the HSPs who struggle and those who do not notice because they are thriving. As she says, there are indeed HSPs everywhere who manage this. One key aspect being choosing. Choosing aspects of our environment. Choosing the right friends, partner, career. Autonomy and self-control seemingly are vital to thriving as an HSP.

Barbara Allen is clear about some of the skills and benefits of being an HSP. HSPs are good at uniting information and ideas, noticing the joins, the in-between things. Which reminds me, a lead we did not follow up in our BBC documentary was with the Scottish police, who reportedly use sensitivity as part of their recruitment and training strategy for senior roles such as detectives, in that they are looking for people able to piece together information and understand connections. I suppose it is partly the skillset that Poirot, Miss Marple and others use. HSPs understand the subtleties, the facets of complexity that form people and situations, including motives and bias. They understand layers of information, can see a bird's-eye view and close detail, and they are drawn to and motivated by meaning, making them excellent people to consult over long-term, considered decision-making. I am haunted by the phrase Barbara Allen used about what mirror neurons are for, in essence what HSPs are for: 'So we don't explode everything.' Aren't we just on the precipice of doing exactly that as a species? It makes me realize how very much we need the skills of HSPs: we need their voices in discussions, we need them at the tables of power along with other types of intelligence. I am struck by Barbara Allen's understanding that HSPs are for responding to others and ourselves and our environment appropriately. I think that is the skill of care and vision. I think about the jobs that entail care and vision in our society, examples being carers, parenting, artists. We treat each of those workers appallingly as a society, with outright contempt – low pay, poor conditions, low esteem, continually on the cutting end of government reform, yet holding up an economy from underneath.

Re-reading the transcript of the interview with Barbara Allen, I realize how much she applies to herself the learning she shared with me. How she sets clear boundaries, prioritizes downtime. It is a good lesson, or rather a reminder of the need to be almost excessively strict with yourself about these things. So, in the name of mirroring the work that Barbara Allen does, with the aim of giving myself flexibility, more autonomy and care, I am going to:

- Plan annual leave in for each year
- Plan to spend more time alone
- Get better at saying no, thank you
- Stop apologizing for zoning out
- Be very careful with the choices I make about who to work with

I think the main challenge of sensitivity is the misunderstanding that comes from seeing overwhelm, a moment of sensory and psychological distress, and thinking that is all sensitivity means and offers. This chapter has taught me that overwhelm is a sign of an HSP not thriving. It has reminded me to implement strategies to offer myself alternatives. I have realized that means speaking up about what I need and not apologizing for it. In the words of my sister Rachel Walker, a great and sensitive woman, 'You cannot successfully learn not to be sensitive, but you can learn tactics to best manage being sensitive.' And talking of learning tactics – I would like to introduce you to the queen of self-management tactics for mental health.

Jess: My name is Jessica O'Garr. I'm a clinical psychologist. I've got a master's degree from the University of Wollongong in Australia. At my day job I work at a private psychiatric facility. I've started a free resource called Psych Collective with Dr Al Griskaitis, who is a consultant psychiatrist. Together we make free mental health resources, YouTube videos, handouts, worksheets for people across nine topics: distress, sleep, trauma, emotions, personality, anxiety, mood, mind and body schema therapy.

We work with a lot of highly sensitive patients. Our attitude is that it's not your fault that you are wired to experience the world this way, and that it is your responsibility to learn strategy to survive in a world that has a lot of stimuli. We acknowledge that you will come up against people who don't get it and don't understand what it is like to be an HSP, and you don't have to educate them. You've just got to survive within yourself. You need to learn how to tolerate your inner

115

world without trying to numb it, push it away or ignore it. Our philosophy is 'skills before pills', because we want people to respond to their emotions skilfully, not just reach for the pills to take the feelings away.

The sensitivity of our temperament is dictated by genetics. We are born with a certain level of sensitivity, which exists on a continuum from low to high. How you learn to manage your sensitivity will largely depend on the type of messaging you were given in your early environment. For example, if a child grows up in an invalidating environment, where they hear messages like 'Stop crying or I will give you something to cry about', 'Stop being a drama queen' or 'Stop being so sensitive', then they will learn that if they show emotion they will be rejected or punished.

Those sorts of messages set up a belief for the child where they think, 'OK, well, Mum and Dad are telling me I'm not supposed to feel this way, so there must be something wrong with me and my feelings.' The child then tries to repress or shut down or detach from their feelings. Which is an unachievable task. Because they cannot succeed in always repressing their emotions, they experience shame. The idea that 'there must be something wrong with me' then becomes the next emotional event that triggers the cycle around again. So, the biggest problem that I see for people with a heightened sensitivity is they've been taught that their heightened sensitivity is a bad thing, and they feel distress about that, and they detest the distress. Whereas what we need them to be able to do is to validate the distress and practise compassion towards themselves in distress.

THE CYCLE OF INVALIDATION

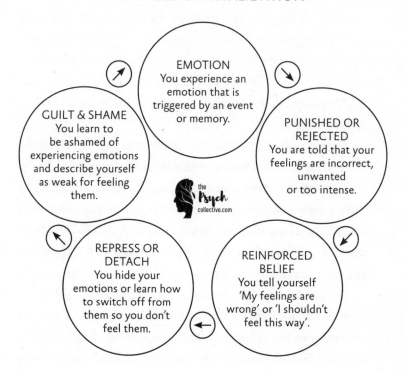

Hannah: That's so interesting. And makes me think back to when I interviewed my mum. I come from a big family of HSPs. Mum grew up in a non-validating environment and then had a lot of kids and sort of made it her mission to create home as a validating environment for them, along with my dad. And that was wonderful, except for our experience of then going out into the world into a non-validating environment – school, workplaces, etc.

Jess: None of my patients would describe the childhood that you've had; they're all coming to me saying, 'I've got these feelings, nobody told me that was OK my whole life. And I hate my feelings now that they are overwhelming, can you teach me how to get rid of my feelings?' And my role is to say no, we cannot delete them, but we can learn skills for how to deal with them.

First, we must help our patients to measure their distress. We use a scale called Subjective Units of Distress, or SUDS for short. It is subjective because each person gets to measure their own distress. No one else gets to tell them how distressed they are. We use a basic one-to-ten scale, where 10/10 is the highest distress, you have ever felt (usually a panic attack for those who have had them) and 1/10 is super-chilled, almost sleepy.

So, if I am sitting on the couch late at night watching Netflix, I'm probably at 2/10. I'm alert enough that I can pay attention to the show, but my body is relaxed and I'm not distressed about anything. Whereas if I am about to walk into a staff meeting where I have to give a big presentation, then I might be at 5/10. This would mean I am feeling the arousal in my body, may be a bit nervous about my presentation, but I am alert and engaged and still able to cope and function. Research shows that a moderate level of arousal is best for peak performance. If you don't care, you won't perform. So, you need to feel something to get results.

The problem starts to occur when distress goes higher than what someone can cope with. Everyone has a tipping point on the SUDS scale where their distress becomes so high that it interferes with functioning. We call this the boiling point. For most people it is around seven or eight. But for HSPs, it could be five or six. Once someone has boiled over, then

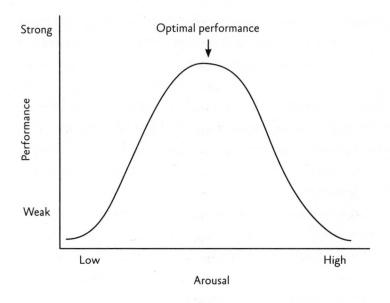

they are outside their window of tolerance, and everything gets harder to manage.

What determines where your boiling point is will depend on two factors: temperament and skills. If you have a highly sensitive temperament, then your boiling point is going to be lower. Stuff that seems small to others will set you off quicker because it feels bigger to you. But you can change that if you have the right skills. HSPs with no skills will tap out lower. They'll reach that threshold sooner where they cannot take in information, can't function, can't think clearly and struggle to make decisions. But once you have skills, then you can tolerate more distress before it becomes overwhelming, so it pushes your boiling point up one or two points, giving you a larger window of tolerance.

Hannah: You have a free resource video that I watched about threat, drive and soothe systems: could you please explain what those are for me?

Jess: The model is developed by Paul Gilbert. I think his early publications are around about 2005 and 2009. So, I've taken his model and connected it together with three different approaches. It starts with a model with three components: threat, drive and soothe.

Now threat is straightforward. It's the limbic system, where the amygdala lives and controls the panic response. It's the part of our brain that is constantly scanning and evaluating for threat. People who've had experiences of trauma, particularly PTSD or complex PTSD, they are going to have a heightened threat system. This is because the brain, in its simplest form, is a survival organ. Its job is to keep itself alive, which is why it manages our autonomic functions of breathing and heart pumping, etc. But it also manages the part of our brain that looks for threats in our environment. Therefore, as humans, we have a natural predisposition to look for the negative and remember the negative more than the positive. So, if I say, 'Tell me about your worst memory in primary school', you will probably be able to recall that faster than you could recall your best memory from primary school. So, what is that? That's a survival technique.

Let's say you put your hand on the stove top and burn yourself. You only have to do that once for your brain to say, 'That hot plate represents danger. Don't do that again.' And your brain will hold on to that memory and, in the case of PTSD, keep reminding you of that memory, so you don't forget the lesson that the stove top is dangerous. But the brain is not only looking out for physical threat, but social threat as well. So 'Remember the time that you were bullied' – that represents danger. Don't put yourself back in that situation because you don't want to experience that threat again. Whereas something like 'Remember the day that your best friend threw you a surprise party', there was no threat in that, so your brain doesn't encode it the same way. So, your threat system is constantly looking for threat and reminding you of previous threats as a warning not to let that happen again. Because the brain thinks that because it happened before it *will* happen again. The threat system is fuelled by adrenaline and cortisol, so the higher your threat prediction, the more adrenaline and cortisol you have flowing through your body, and that is not good.

Hannah: And what is the next system?

Jess: We also have a drive system. Our drive system exists to seek out resources and productivity – it's the part of us that gets stuff done; when we are not threatened, then we can be driven. It is about being task-focused, productive and achieving. It runs on dopamine. The drive system prompts us to do anything: clean the house, clean ourselves, look after our children, complete tasks, see friends, achieve at work, make money. We need our drive system.

The problem occurs when people try to use their drive system when they are outside of their window of tolerance. So often I see patients trying to 'fix' their distress or threat system. They want to solve the problem of distress by ignoring it, repressing it or trying to take it away with drugs, alcohol, shopping, eating, overworking or overscheduling. It just doesn't work. This is when people hit burnout or breakdown. They blame themselves for failing, beat themselves up for not being 'strong enough' and consider emotions as failure. Then they are back into their threat system.

So, when you are within your window of tolerance (below your boiling point), then you need your drive system. Because you need to go to work, you need to be productive. Even if you're staying at home, you need to cook, you need to clean, you need to organize the house, you need to manage the kids, you need to exercise, you need to make sure you're making healthy food choices. And all of that comes from the drive system. But once you are outside your window of tolerance, you need your soothe system.

The soothe system is our care system. It promotes bonding, helps us manage stress by intentionally and deliberately engaging in self-care.

The soothe system is not designed to take away our distress (or threat), but rather it allows us to look after ourselves while we experience the distress. Now let's be clear, your soothe system should not be used when there is actual threat. If you really are in danger, use your threat system to motivate you to run away. That is what it is there for. But if the threat is perceived, or if the threat is psychological (such as feeling overwhelmed by too many tasks at work), then you need to use your soothe system to take care of your distress until you can get back into your window of tolerance, and then you can re-engage your drive system.

Most of my patients have an underdeveloped soothe system. So, they often get stuck ping-ponging between the threat system and the drive system because their soothe system is absent.

Let me give you an example. Let's say my biggest threat is fear of failure. Failure is a big social and psychological threat. So, to try and fix that, I will overcompensate by trying to be perfect, because if I am perfect, I can avoid the threat. So, all my energy from my drive system goes into making sure I show up at work at 7am and stay until 10pm, anticipating everything the boss is going to need before they know they need it, dotting all the I's, and crossing all the T's. Everything is always done, and everything is always perfect. I feel safe from the threat of failure.

The trouble is, this is not sustainable. At some point, I'll hit burnout. And when you burn out, you cannot perform well and you fall back into the threat system and, on top of that, you feel ashamed about it.

Hannah: When you're describing that I keep imagining a small creature trying to scramble out of a mud pit by climbing up the bank, and they keep sliding back in.

Jess: The soothe system is vastly underrated and used by most of us. I often ask patients to think about those three systems, and to think about roughly how much time they think they spend in each of those systems, as a percentage. I recommend a split between 60/30/10, and they say, 'Yeah, 60 per cent threat, 30 per cent drive and 10 per cent soothe.' I say, 'No! 60 per cent drive, 30 per cent soothe and 10 per cent threat' and they are gobsmacked.

Hannah: Do you think highly sensitive people are particularly prone to getting stuck between those two systems?

Jess: Yes, I do. And a lot of that depends on their early environment, how were they taught to respond to themselves. Did they have a parent who says, 'I can see you're exhausted, take a break, come sit down and have a hug' or 'Let's just chill for a bit and we'll come back to this later'? Or did they have a parent who said, 'You've got to get that assignment done; just keep pushing through it' or 'Stop being so sensitive'? What was prioritized? Performance or emotion? And what was punished? Was the expression of emotion punished? Was the child left thinking, 'Mum doesn't like it when I cry, so I'd better not cry.' Because the child's feeling does not go anywhere. That instinct to cry, it is just turned in on themselves and shamed. Were they validated or invalidated when expressing how they felt? That really matters.

This has a huge impact on how we then manage our emotions as an adult. How we talk to and treat ourselves when we are at boiling point is important. Do you think, 'Oh my God, I've got so much to do, I must keep going, I can't stop. I'm exhausted, but I have to keep going'? And then crash? And then once you've crashed on the couch, are you physically resting but psychologically thinking, 'I cannot believe I didn't get it all done'? Are you kicking yourself, guilting yourself, flogging yourself? Telling yourself that you cannot rest, you must get this done, even if you are exhausted? That is a crash cycle. That is overuse of the drive function.

However, if we learn the skill of identifying early-warning signs and catch ourselves, then we can take steps to avoid crashing. Instead of ignoring early-warning signs, crashing and being down for a week, we could mindfully choose to turn on our soothe system. A lot of people have resistance to using this system. Their internal messaging will be telling

THE CRASH CYCLE

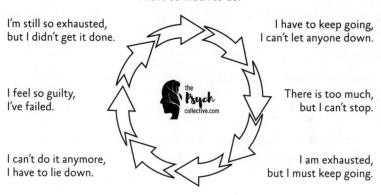

Oh my gosh,
I have so much to do.

I have to keep going,
I can't let anyone down.

There is too much,
but I can't stop.

I am exhausted,
but I must keep going.

I can't do it anymore,
I have to lie down.

I feel so guilty,
I've failed.

I'm still so exhausted,
but I didn't get it done.

them, from early childhood usually, 'I'm not allowed to take care of my feelings, I have to push through my feelings.' That can be hard to work through. But we all, regardless of whether we're sensitive or not, need to get better at using our soothe system. The soothe system needs to come with permission to look after yourself. It is a skill to learn. Once we can recognize the warning signs that indicate we are near a crash, we can engage what I call the planned recovery cycle instead. Planned recovery is about deliberately scheduling time for self-care and rest in among all the other tasks we must get done. It staves off burnout and promotes soothing.

If you weren't raised in an environment that promoted self-care, then you will need to intentionally learn how to do it. Let me talk you through the four components of emotional wellbeing.

PLANNED RECOVERY

Oh my gosh,
I have so much to do.

Okay, let's break this
down into chunks.

I am going to get
X and Y done,
then I will rest.

That took a lot of effort,
I need a break.

I will have a rest and do
something relaxing
for 30 min.

I have given myself
permission for this
so I don't feel guilty.

I feel restored and ready
for the next task

1. **Self-care** is about looking after the basics. Make sure you eat right, sleep well and move regularly. It is about hygiene and grooming and avoiding substances like drugs and alcohol.

2. **Self-validation** is about acknowledging your inner experiences as real for you. It is not asking you to like them, or even to want them. You just must accept that they are there. Self-validation sounds like, 'My feelings are real for me. I am struggling. I am in distress. I feel scared.'

3. **Self-soothing** is about looking after yourself while you feel distress. It is about the actions that you take to care for yourself, with the aim of reducing the intensity of the distress. We often use the five senses for this, so think about what is soothing to look at (photos, scenery, TV), to listen to (music, nature sounds, binaural beats), to smell

(candles, flowers, body cream), to taste (tea, mints, juice) and touch (weighted blanket, warm shower, hoodie). These self-soothing behaviours need to be familiar, comfortable, known and authentic.

4. **Self-compassion** is the willingness to look after yourself with kindness while you experience your feelings. It says, 'I deserve to look after myself while I am feeling distressed.' It says, 'That was a really hard day, I struggled with that, and now I am going to take care of myself while I recover from my day and let my big feelings pass.' It is empowering to know and feel that you can look after yourself while you're having these feelings, talking to yourself with kindness, not pretending the threat is not happening, but holding yourself with compassion, having the skills to look after yourself.

Hannah: It makes me a little bit tearful to hear you explain that. The idea of being kind to yourself while you feel in distress instead of thinking, well, you shouldn't be distressed. It is very caring to yourself. That is what I hope for my daughter, I think that might be the very centre of the reason I am writing this book. I want her to be able to be kind to herself. I have spent so much of my life being so unkind to myself. I want something different for her. I want her to be able to validate herself.

Jess: Validation is about acknowledging the experience instead of denying it, looking at it instead of ignoring it. Compassion is about our internal voice and how kind it is to us. The skills are in learning how to treat ourselves. If patients really struggle with that, I ask them to think about how they would respond if it was someone they loved. Then I ask them to apply that to themselves. And though we can ask others to help us with our self-compassion, as in you can ask for compassion from others, it is no one else's responsibility, you must learn the skills for yourself. It is no one else's job to provide those things for you.

Maintaining these skills also takes a lot of boundaries. HSPs struggle with boundaries, they take on other people's feelings, they try to help others. And what that can mean is that the space which should be filled with self-care is filled with caring for others. And it causes emotional burnout – you have given away your tolerance capacity.

For example, if you usually have a set time on a Saturday morning for exercise, and someone asks, 'Can you babysit my kids instead?', what do you do? People with low boundaries will give in and do what others want. But there is no skill in giving in. The skill is in protecting your time for self-care. You need to find a way to set a boundary that says, I need this time, I am going to protect it.

Another example is when someone says, 'Tell me what it was like growing up in your home, when you were a kid.' Well, you get to decide how much of that you want to share. That's a boundary. Or what if people are being critical, how do you respond to that? Do you say, 'I'm not comfortable when you speak to me that way' or do you stay silent? What do you allow? What do you protect? Where are your boundaries?

Hannah: Yes, I have a big problem with that. If someone asks me a favour, even if it really imposes on my time, I say yes. I struggle with saying no, I feel guilty.

Jess: One of the biggest things I see with my HSP patients is distress intolerance, which is an unwillingness to tolerate distress. If you have a hypersensitive temperament, you feel things more intensely. We use the analogy of it's like having a peanut allergy without an epi pen. So HSPs get these massive reactions and are probably lacking the skills (the epi pen) to take the edge off. So, they are just left in this state of psychological anaphylaxis. And that isn't comfortable. No one wants to feel like that, so they will do what they can to avoid those feelings.

So, when a threat is detected – and HSPs are good at detecting threat – they detect it, feel the discomfort, have an emotional and possibly physical response, and try to get away from the threat and discomfort. They go through a process of trying to shut it down, numbing, dissociating or simply avoiding any situation that could bring on the big feelings, and then they will get smaller in themselves. So, although it seems like the solution is to avoid the distress, distress intolerance is never going to be the solution for managing your emotions – hiding them, burying them, detaching from them, deleting them, it's never going to work. HSPs need to learn how to regulate their emotions, by first allowing themselves to feel them.

You've got to have the willingness to experience that vulnerability that comes with feeling. And it may be that you will have people in your life who can't handle your feelings. People who tell you that you are too sensitive. What they are really telling you is that they can't handle your sensitivity. And you must think, 'Thank you very much for making your position clear.' Now you know not to rely on them for emotional support.

So, we want to swap distress intolerance for distress tolerance, which is accepting your emotions and making some space for them. First, acknowledge the distress and then, secondly, respond to the distress. Start by noticing, where do you feel the feeling in your body? How are you showing it to others? What's your facial expression? What's your body language? Then notice the urge. Every emotion has an action urge, the function of emotion is to motivate you towards action.

Then choose to respond to the emotion. You need to choose to regulate yourself. Are you going to soothe the emotion by using your five senses, or do you need to discharge the emotion by talking, crying, journaling, screaming into a pillow, punching a punching bag, shaking or running? Next, choose how you will respond to those urges you just noticed. If the urge will lead to something harmful or regrettable, do the opposite. Use self-compassion instead of self-harm. Say no instead of giving in. Ask for what you need instead of staying silent. And be kind to yourself while you're doing it. This will take practice.

Remember: if you always do what you've always done, you'll always get what you've always got. So go do it differently.

The idea that your nature is not your fault, but that it is your responsibility to learn to tolerate your inner world without pushing it away is to me both tender and practical. Talking to Jessica O'Garr made me realize what an underdeveloped soothe system I have, and I think I am not alone in that. I realize that my experience of being very sensitive has always been characterized by overwhelm and trying to get away from the distress. And I think that is what my mum has too. The idea of not trying to take the distress away, but rather of looking after ourselves while we experience the distress, feels radical and makes me want to cry a bit – it's so kind, it's so parental. And then suddenly I realize, I don't think I love myself enough, or rather, I don't think my character or traits, my sensitivity, has value. I apply brutal conditions to myself that I would not do to others, I have taught myself that success looks like self-toughness. That self-compassion means weakness.

How we learn to respond to ourselves is so crucial, shapes so much of how we navigate the world, and if you were taught to respond negatively to yourself, perhaps it's not too late to begin to change that. Speaking to Jessica O'Garr reminded me once again of the vital nature of considerate parenting. It reminded me of what my mum said about parenting a highly sensitive child: 'It's like stroking feathers that have been pushed in all the wrong directions. Like detangling your child's hair when it's knotted in the morning. Soothe them...'

We all need validation, all of us, and highly sensitive children need to be validated in their emotional expression. We all benefit from considering what is prioritized: performance or emotion. The idea of 'How would you respond if it was someone you loved?' reaches right into me. I think of how I talk to myself when I am in distress. I use language like 'Tough it out, come on, push through it.' It makes me think of the nickname, Knuckles, that I earned from my friends. The idea of treating yourself with compassion, or radical softness, is refreshing. And makes me realize yet another tension HSPs often exist within: great compassion and understanding for others, and not so much for ourselves. If it was my mum, I would sit down next to her, and be alongside while she was in distress, let her know that she was heard and loved. If it was my daughter, I would pick her up and hold her and sit her down somewhere where we could look each other in the face and ask her how she was feeling, what was causing her distress and I would listen and validate while she expressed herself. I would say, 'Yes, that sounds really hard. What can I do to help you?'

If you have difficulty practising self-compassion, imagine responding to yourself as if it was someone you love. I am sure that you, like me, can think of a time, or many times, in your life when you have overcome your emotional response to achieve something. It feels great, you are so surprised at yourself. But what if you get stuck in that mode? What if you get stuck in thinking, to have value, to have worth, I have to override how I am feeling? I think that is very dangerous. And I think it has implications broader than the impact on the individual. Like Barbara Allen said; take something out of the system in the wild and it has a big impact. Do we as a species, as individuals, need to learn to be radically soft, do we need to learn to hold our vulnerability as a thing of beauty and potential, not of weakness? As Jessica O'Garr said, 'You have got to be willing to experience the vulnerability that comes with feeling.'

I totally understand the instinct to armour up. It's so tempting, isn't it? American academic Brené Brown talks about this, how sometimes we need to put on armour to go out and do our jobs and be in the world. And how sometimes when we come home, it's easier to keep that armour on instead of taking it off. What that means is we start to lose something of ourselves, something important in connection, something fundamental about being human.

The story of sensitivity in this chapter has got a little broader, I feel. Being highly sensitive often comes with a wide variety of challenges. To navigate the world in which we live, to manage ourselves, requires significant upskilling and taking of responsibility. HSPs are always taking in a lot of information. I think that has significance, because what it means is that those who are more sensitive are more likely to have quality data (emotional and factual) about any given interpersonal situation or environment. And though that comes with significant challenges – what a gift for us all to have in our midst. We have this type of human who is super paying attention. Super attention-payers. Highly considered response people. I think of the sum that Barbara Allen mentioned – when empathy collides with a belief system it provokes action. I think we are starting to really excavate the meaning of sensitivity. I am starting to understand it as a resource – possibly one that can help us move forwards with responsible, skilled, active response. I leave this chapter, and this section of the book, with Barbara Allen's words ringing in my head: 'Every response is designed for the survival of the species.'

Part 2
Changing the Story

6. Sensitivity and the past

The first half of this book has focused on the story we currently hold about sensitivity. In the main, we do not consider it to be useful or valuable. I am curious to know if this has always been the case. If there were different understandings of sensitivity in the past. How to find out? Conveniently, I am married to Dr Oscar Aldred, an archaeologist who knows a lot of people in interconnecting fields. This is the chapter that, when I started working on the book, I felt most concerned and excited by. Concerned because I did not know if I would find the right people to talk to. Excited because thinking about versions of us outside of the time we are living in right now is really exciting. How did people in the past construct value? Where and who held meaning and status? These are things I love to talk about because we learn so much about us now by looking back.

My partner is not a conventionally romantic man. But when he goes on walks, which is often, he is always looking on the ground or into the distance. And he always finds something that most of us would have overlooked. He brings these home for me – little bits of Roman pot, fossils, hand-worked flints – and presses them into my hand. Sometimes there are fingerprints in the clay that make up the pot. 'Bit of a dead person's pot,' we joke. I keep them on a shelf at home – our collection of dead people's things. I don't find this morbid, these bits of pots from dead people's houses; it's a reminder that we are standing on the shoulders of so many people who have come before us. That our time is here, now, and that it too shall pass. It's a reminder that we are living within a specific moment of time, which to us seems the way life has always been. But in fact that is quite untrue. There have been and are many forms of societies. We in the West are currently living in a society governed by the principle of commerce. As I touched on in chapter 4, the system of education was developed to suit the needs of a changing economy, that of industrialization. There is much debate about how far back capitalism goes, because it takes so many forms. I'm not going to enter that particular arena, because it's contentious, so let's just say there was a time in our past when we existed prior to industrialism and capitalism.

When examining past societies, it is difficult to read their values, because except for written accounts, primarily by white men, what remain are mainly material objects. And that is why when I began this search, after my husband had given me a list of museum directors, I immediately came up against dead ends. I received kind, swift answers such as, 'Thank you for your interesting and pertinent enquiry, we are really interested in this subject. However, we look at the micro of the objects within our collection, so the relationship to understanding the macro of their significance among a value system that might be different to our own is not something we can offer currently.'

To be honest, I found this frustrating. Isn't that the point of examining past societies? To understand what and who they were? I had naively believed that I might be able to find some museum object/s that illustrated something about the past and a different order of values. And I hoped to find that specific object connection because it's concrete, we can see it.

Many of us have this experience, perhaps self-created, when we visit museums. For example, I remember seeing the antler headdresses in the Star Carr exhibition at the Cambridge Museum of Archaeology and Anthropology. Star Carr is a Mesolithic (Middle Stone Age, dating to around 9000 BC) archaeological site in North Yorkshire. I was facilitating a Writing the Past workshop for young people from a Cambridge school. Together, the teacher, the pupils and I walked around the exhibition, which was multisensory, with boxes you could open and sniff, tree bark and fabric to touch, a soundscape to move around to, and dimmed lights. Because it was sensory, it felt enveloping and absorbing. The display explained that the environment at Star Carr had increasingly become affected by gradual but dramatic climate change. The temperature dropped, the lake became shallower and swampier, and though dwellers adapted throughout decades, they were eventually forced to relocate.

Many artefacts were found well preserved due to being buried deep within the peat. Among the finds were twenty-one deer-antler headdresses. Or antler frontlets, as is their proper name. The curator escorting us around the exhibition stopped in front of the cabinet containing the largest headdress, standing right in front of it, so the antlers rose out of the top of her head. She looked otherworldly.

'In an environment under threat, what do you think these frontlets were for?' she asked the group.

The twelve-year-olds were silent. One child raised their hand: 'To pretend to be like deer?'

'Yes, that is right! Maybe! We cannot absolutely know,' said the curator. 'We don't entirely know – we can never entirely know, we are people living in the times and world we do now, with the understanding and ideas we have now, so everything we pass backwards is a projection of our times. *But* we can make a series of interpretations. We can assume that once a person is wearing the antlers you look and perhaps feel more like a deer. Now what is that for? Could be as simple as, for hunting deer. But when we consider this was an environment under threat, with land disappearing, it could be a kind of ritual practice. It could be a form of shamanism, an attempt to connect with the natural world.'

Shamanism is a practice where someone, or some people, interact through altered consciousness with the goal of directing different energies. Could it be that those antler frontlets were a way of using sensitivity? As in, people had noticed their environment was changing, deer symbolized a good source of food, or simply energy, and wearing the frontlets while conducting ritual was a way of trying to communicate with energies surrounding them. Something bigger than themselves. An understanding that there are other things in the world than humans, that we are a part of a whole.

There are many past societies with evidence of shamanistic ritual, in a wide range of forms; in fact this is still an ongoing practice in some indigenous communities. An attempt to connect outside of ourselves with something, whether that be a deity, a landscape, our ancestors, an animal. These practices are a topic of much debate and multiple interpretation. Professor Roger Walsh discusses the skills needed for shamanic roles in his paper 'The Making of a Shaman: Calling, Training and Culmination', explaining that they are 'said to sometimes include talents such as heightened sensitivity and perception'. The text goes on to say that shamans 'are said to commonly display remarkable energy and stamina, unusual levels of concentration, control of altered states of consciousness, high intelligence, leadership skills, and a grasp of complex data, myths, and rituals'.

Reading that list, it is not a long jump to the skills of the highly sensitive – deep noticing, information-holding and knitting, quiet leadership, story-holding, place-making.

My partner has a lot of books. A lot. Among his vast collection, one name comes up time and time again, anthropologist Professor Tim Ingold. I have heard my partner refer to him in a wide range of contexts to illustrate a discussion about contemporary and historical periods and understandings. When I asked him who I should contact to get a better insight into what was valued by society in the past, he gave me the email address of Dr Jo Vergunst, senior lecturer and head of the anthropology department at the University of Aberdeen. In response to my email request, Jo kindly shared an article by – you guessed it – Professor Tim Ingold.

Professor Ingold's paper, 'Dreaming of Dragons: On the Imagination of Real Life', explores the rupture between the real world and our imagination of it. He uses the idea of nature as being like a book that people read from:

> The idea of the book of nature, however, dates
> from medieval times. For medieval readers as for
> indigenous hunters, creatures would speak and offer
> counsel. But in the transition to modernity the book
> was silenced.

He explains that we have shifted away from a culture whereby humans read the environment, connecting outside of simply human self and rational thought and knowledge, and goes on to discuss the impact that the advancement of science and known quantified knowledge had on imagination and connection to forces outside of our known human world. In fact, he makes the case that we are now all born into a system that educates us on the authority of scientific knowns. He is at pains to ensure we understand that he considers scientific knowns to be valuable, but that this need not be at the cost of other types of connection and knowing:

> How can we make a space for art and literature, for religion, or for the beliefs and practices of indigenous peoples, in an economy of knowledge in which the search for the true nature of things has become the exclusive prerogative of rational science?

This monopoly of understanding towards the sciences does indeed come at a cost and, I think, is strongly connected to the devaluing of the trait and skills of the highly sensitive. Highly sensitive people are connecting all the time with energy around them, their nervous systems are built that way. It is therefore not a stretch to imagine back in time to cultures where multiple types of reading and understanding were part of human experience: the sort of understanding offered by religious leaders, storytellers, nature deep-noticers and practitioners, and many more. In very simple terms, our survival was much more dependent on paying attention to nature and things greater than the human world, because of food, water, security. We are largely deeply disconnected from those things now. Ways of noticing were useful for individuals and the group, inherited knowledge and noticing. Professor Ingold argues that we have in the main forgotten ways of listening outside of ourselves:

...as philosopher Stephen Vogel (2006) observes, the
world of nature abounds in movement and gesture,
much of which is manifested as sound: think of
the clap of thunder and the howling of the wind,
the cracking of ice and the roar of the waterfall, the
rustling of trees and the calls of birds.

Nature and the environment are talking to us all the time. HSPs
are extremely likely to notice and be profoundly affected by
environment and the information being communicated within
it. But the value we give to that skill has diminished. The ability
to read between the lines of nature, to understand more than the
human world – we dismiss that as mumbo jumbo.

I decided to email Professor Tim Ingold, thinking there was
not a chance he would get back to me – he is a big, big name and
very busy. The next morning, I walked to work, working on a
Saturday, my husband taking care of our daughter. My office is in
the centre of town, where there is a weekend market. It's an old
market. My sister has recently set up a business to support herself
and her two daughters, selling baskets from around the world. She
is a great saleswoman, calls everyone darling, and from my desk
with the window open I can hear her charming people, telling
them about the origins of the baskets, the communities that have
made them. I checked my email midday and to my amazement
Professor Ingold had emailed me back. He directed me to a paper
due to be published late 2021, in a book called *Imagining for Real
– Essays on Creation, Attention and Correspondence*. The paper he
shared with me was called 'The World in a Basket'. As I opened
the article, I heard my sister tell a customer, 'Yes, the baskets take
a long time to be made, that one is banana leaf.'

In his paper, Tim Ingold uses the metaphor of skills involved in the creation of baskets to explore how life used to be lived, and how it is lived now. He draws on the image of fibres from plant stalks being bound together to create a rope from which communities weave baskets, a rope that connects generations in the past to ones in the future. The making of a basket has a rhythm, skills, stories which are embodied within that community; the making explores a connection to landscape, people, time, identity:

> For there is much more to weaving baskets than mere technique. It is a life process. Its generativity lies in the unfolding of an entire field of vital relations wherein not only things, but also people and their provisions, are as much grown as made. Like the twisting of cords from which baskets are very often (though not universally) constructed, weaving closely models social life. People would bring the same tactile sensibility, the same sense of movement and pattern, into the choreography of their lives with one another as into that of their hands in working with materials. Every basket can be compared to a little community, binding its constituent fibres, as the community binds lives, into a supple and durable form. Like the community in its classical sense of 'giving-together' (from the Latin, *com*, 'together', plus *munus*, 'gift'), the basket is not closed in on itself but open-ended: open to others, to the past and to the future. And as communities produce baskets, so baskets reproduce communities. For in the practice of the craft, basketry produces its makers as well as the things themselves, building a feel for the work into their muscle memory, sense of rhythm and perceptual attunement.

Professor Ingold goes on to make the point that throughout history, the young have grown in a culture that teaches them stories and to observe the practices of their elders. When we shifted into education provided by the state, 'information' came to mean known scientific knowledge, so the stories and craft were eliminated: 'The spinning of fibres, once a ubiquitous task of daily life, has largely become confined as a niche art for hobbyists and the purveyors of heritage, and as spun cord disappears from common use, so records have ceased to be stories to tell and to follow.'

The importance of transmitting information from one generation to the next, through craft, place and storytelling, is stressed here as a key characteristic of the past. Professor Ingold asks if balance and diversity can be restored, can we think outside the strictures of power and connection we currently hold?

> I believe this can be done, but only by restoring ways of telling, currently relegated to the peripheries of social life, to its very core. This entails a renewed focus on the practices of craft, and on the stories and skills they engender. Of all human crafts, the interweaving of flexible cords, wickers, or roots to form containers, traps, cages, hats, and a host of other everyday utensils is perhaps the most ancient and widespread, as common to humans as nest-building is to birds.

I return to what Barbara Allen said: 'It's innate in sensitive people, the ability to see the bigger picture – an awareness that there are communities and environments out there bigger than you and that we are connected.' So, did we understand the value of sensitivity differently in the past? Was it one of the things that helped keep a society glued together?

How to begin answering that? Nature was a book we read from. We listened in a different way to different things. Creatures, even, in some cases and in many stories. We, as beings, engaged in communication in multiple directions. I have realized there is a key new understanding here, important to answering the question of whether sensitivity was valued differently in the past. That new understanding is the difference between skill and trait. HSPs have more of the *trait* of sensitivity. But we are all born with a set of instincts, we have the capacity to learn the *skill* of sensitivity. The culture we live in teaches us specific skills. Skills considered useful to the time in which we live. Skills that we either develop or do not. Sensitivity is a skill we all have access to, that historically we have been dependent on. As Tim Ingold explains, skills such as basket-making involve entanglement with the environment, entanglement of identity, rhythm, survival, community structure. The Star Carr finds (see page 139) may show us a group of people trying to take on the power of connecting outside themselves to something larger – in this case, becoming deer. Each of these things requires a set of skills – taking care, noticing, empathy, storytelling, cooperation, understanding, considered decision-making. Each of those are subset skills that require the use of sensitivity. And that skill was vital in the past, not just for us individually, but for whole societal structures. We have lived in a way that requires us to think about our connection to things other than ourselves, to nature, to ancestors, to future generations, to our community, to the past and to the future. To live in balance with environment requires the skill of sensitivity – to hold the idea of ourselves as part of something. We currently hold nature as something we operate on top of, something that is there to charm us, to be made something of, light entertainment and resource that goes on around our real lives. We have lost our understanding of what we are part of, the need for humility and reverence, the exchange, the noticing of danger. Historically we are interwoven with environment, resources, each other, weaving modelling our social life as well. This is the past, for all of us. So was sensitivity valued differently in the past? Yes, in an intrinsically different way. A way that it is not too late to learn how to listen to once more.

And as for the question, would highly sensitive people have been valued differently in the past? Who knows? What I do know is that a society gives value to the people who best match the values of the time they are living in. And we have not always lived in a society that prioritized bigger, better, more. We have lived in times that found sensitivity and its parts to be of value. We have lived in a way that required the skills of sensitivity, knowing how to read nature and people as a book. How to be part of, rather than apart. We are reading environment all the time, all of us, above and in our conscious minds. I think of Tim Ingold's description, 'It is the time of weather and the seasons, of breaking waves and running rivers, of the growth and decay of vegetation and the coming and going of animals, of breaths and heartbeats.' The ability to read all this information, to listen and make considered decisions to react appropriately, as part of something bigger than ourselves, is in us all as a skill that we have the potential to develop. The name of that skill is sensitivity. And what valuable potential it holds, what resource and what great distance it has carried us, so far.

7. How did you know?

I want to learn more about a key area of high sensitivity, an area deprioritized by our current understanding of what constitutes reliable information – knowing and sensing. Empathy is the ability to understand and share the feelings of another. Of course, none of us can entirely know how another person feels. In fact, 'I know how you feel' may well be up there as one of the most insensitive statements one person can make to another. It makes the other person feel as if you are comparing their experience to your own, as if you are claiming their experience. I am not talking about that aspect of 'I know how you feel', not compared experience. I want to know more about empathy.

Empathy is different from sympathy. Sympathy is saying, 'I am so sorry that happened,' feeling sympathetic to the other person. Empathy is feeling what another is feeling, being in the soup with them. Empathy is having the same level of excitement as the friend telling you they are getting married. Empathy is knowing what it is like to lose a parent, too. I have heard that HSPs have exceptionally strong empathy skills. I want to know if this is true. Is there any science behind it? What is it useful for? And what does it do to our understanding of sensitivity?

In 2011, Chris Thorpe and I made a show called *The Oh*

Fuck Moment and took it to the Edinburgh Fringe. It was a show set around an office table, in a regular office, for an audience of twenty-five. We sat at the table with the audience, and throughout the performance we told them stories and poems and asked them to write things down on post-it notes and read them out. The show was about fucking up and how we handle our mistakes. It was about the misappropriated shame attached to mistake-making and how we run our companies as if making a mistake is the worst thing we can do, covering those mistakes up instead of learning from them. Culture has moved on since we made that show (though not because of us), and I think we are all now much more aware of the potential to learn from mistakes. In the show we shared stories of times when Chris and I had each fucked up: Chris missing his father's death after weeks spent waiting in a hospice, me accidentally sending an offensive email to a colleague.

We did the show a lot, often three times a day, to get enough of an audience to meet box-office need. We toured it a lot, for quite a long time. Each audience was unique, of course, because each audience was made of different people, all of whom had different dynamics with each other. Sometimes people came with their friends, sometimes alone, sometimes in couples, sometimes with colleagues. Because of this, and because we were asking them to volunteer information about their lives, each show was different, flavoured by the audience's connection to the material. For example, we always knew if we had an audience member who had, like Chris, missed the final moment of a loved one's life, because their whole-body language changed, and there was an emotional intensity in the room above and beyond that of the story Chris was telling. We could see the audience's faces and reactions up close. In the dressing room after the show,

Chris and I would often chat about the uniqueness of that show. Sometimes it was light craft, sometimes there was a sticking point. Often our conversation would go something like this:

———————————

Hannah: Did you notice that couple were clearly on a date? He was so pleased with himself for being at a piece of theatre, she was mortified at being that close to performers and being asked to participate. Throughout the show she decided she was not going to go on another date with him, that it was not a fit.

Or did you notice the woman who was brimming with grief? She was so upset. I think she lost someone and missed the last moments of their life too.

Chris: Yeah, I noticed she did not want to participate/I noticed she was upset.

Hannah: I could really feel the awkwardness of the couple/the woman who was overflowing with grief.

Chris: I think you are doing a different job to me, maybe.

Hannah: No, I don't think so. I am performing the show. I am doing my job.

Chris: There is a difference between noticing what someone seems to be feeling and knowing what they feel. You seem to be thinking that you can feel what they feel.

Hannah: It does feel like it. I can feel some of what they are feeling.

———————————

These conversations would always feel like we were hitting on a source of friction that neither of us could quite pinpoint or name. Sometimes I would tell him I had felt the whole show, that the collective dynamic had taken on a whole shape of feeling that funnelled in some places and expanded in others. Some shows were bumpy with joy, carried along by the emotion of the audience, while others were introspective, with the audience reflective. Often after the show I would be exhausted and get under the desk and fall asleep. Sometimes I would even do this between shows, napping briefly before waking up to welcome the audience in for the next one. This was the only way I could do the work. Chris knew this and would leave me to it or would work quietly on his laptop in the corner of the room.

Chris and I still talk about that shared experience. We often ask ourselves the question – how come we were both having such different responses to the same show, when our job was the same, we were in the same room and we had both written and were performing the show? Is there some sort of internal difference in our experience? Are we taking in different levels of information? What this experience with Chris revealed to me is that we are two people, doing the same thing but doing it differently, with different results. When I was growing up, part of my confusion about the world was based on being bewildered by others' actions and intentions. I used to think, 'Doesn't that person realize that action hurts that other person? Doesn't that person think about the emotional impact on that other person?' I thought we were all the same, and so I was really confused by how people chose to be. However, research suggests that we may in fact not all be the same in terms of our empathic skills. To investigate this further, I would like to introduce you to one of the key scientific researchers into sensitivity –

Dr Bianca Acevedo. Dr Acevedo has collaborated with Dr Elaine Aron on several key pieces of research.

Bianca: My name is Bianca Acevedo, and I'm a researcher in the Department of Psychological and Brain Sciences at the University of California, Santa Barbara.

Hannah: Thank you. And could you please tell us a bit about your research into sensitivity?

Bianca: Of course. Along with my collaborators, Doctors Elaine and Art Aron, and others, we've conducted some neuroimaging studies on sensitivity and response. For example, in one study we showed these individuals images of their spouses and strangers displaying some sort of emotional response. They were told, 'Your partner is feeling very happy because something wonderful has happened to them' or 'Your partner's feeling very sad, because something terrible has happened to them.' We also showed them images of strangers experiencing happiness and sadness, and while they were looking at these images, we scanned their brains using neuroimaging, MRI. And we looked at their brain activation associated with their sensitivity scores, measured with the classic HSP Scale by Dr Elaine Aron. The more sensitive individuals showed greater activation in the brain, and response to partners' emotional displays. They also showed more activity in areas associated with planning and integration of information from multisensory modalities.

Hannah: So what the study showed was that the brains of the highly sensitive showed more response to partners' and strangers' emotions. And more response in the area of the brain that combines information from sensory sources.

Bianca: Yes. Highly sensitive individuals' brains show greater responsiveness to others' emotions. We also saw activation in areas that are important for integration of information for various sensory modalities, as well as in premotor areas that are involved in the planning of behaviour. Planning is behaviour, that's interesting, so it's pre pre thought before taking an action, which is obviously sensible in any situation. Another very interesting thing that we found across the studies is that in response to positive stimuli, the more sensitive individuals showed greater activation in areas that are related to reward.

Hannah: Meaning that not only did the highly sensitive individuals show more response in relation to negative stimuli, but they equally showed more response to positive stimuli?

Bianca: Yes. These subcortical areas are deeply embedded in our brain and are involved in basic processes related to survival, like looking for food or mating. So, it's not only that highly sensitive people respond to threat in the environment or are overwhelmed by too many things, but they are also vulnerable to the positive things in their environment as well. And we see this concretely in the brain.

Hannah: You have already answered this, but can I dig a bit further into what you think the function of highly sensitive people is to the group?

Bianca: A lot of this research suggests that they are deep integrators of information, connectors, very responsive to other people's emotion and other people's emotional displays. And this serves a species function. They may facilitate cooperation and care and planning in the species. They are more attuned to environment; they may provide society with a different perspective than less sensitive people. The societal implications of being sensitive to others and the environment are that they are able to integrate information deeply, provide deep perspectives on things, and engage in multisensory information-processing to provide appropriate response to another person or the environment.

Hannah: So potentially, they're quite useful?

Bianca: Yes, and in happy situations as well.

Hannah: What is the role of mirror neurons?

Bianca: A mirror neuron is a neuron that fires both when a human acts and when the human observes the same action performed by another. Thus, the neuron 'mirrors' the behaviour of the other, as though the observer were itself acting. We have seen more activation in mirror neurons as a function of high sensitivity.

Hannah: What do you think it must be like to be a highly sensitive person living now in the current world?

Bianca: I think it is becoming increasingly challenging for us all, but particularly for highly sensitive people. Our environment is rapidly changing, and we are all becoming more aware of that. And we have increasing demands on our system because of these changes – technological changes, environmental changes and social changes. So, for everybody, I think we are coping with all these events, and being highly sensitive adds a layer of challenge.

Hannah: I really wanted to ask you a little more about what your views are as to the value of sensitivity to society.

Bianca: Responsiveness. They show activation in areas related to motor activity. So, the premotor areas in several different studies of sensory processing show greater activation for those that are highly sensitive. Though additionally, and seemingly contradictorily, they can seem like they're cautious if something is new. They observe before acting, and that can be very useful to a group, because they're integrating information so that they can respond, hopefully appropriately. So, even in times of stress, they can be a valuable resource. It's useful, as difficult, unknown situations emerge, to have reactive people who observe before participating. And their capacity for empathy means that they are more prone to reflecting instead of judging.

Hannah: What is the function to the group of feeling the feelings of others to a greater degree?

Bianca: Appropriate response and the preparedness to respond, and then not judging but understanding. I'm not saying that all highly sensitive people are peacemakers, because maybe some of them aren't. We need all sorts of temperaments and personalities to make up an effective society.

Hannah: I suppose it's that canary in the coalmine thing too. It's useful to have somebody among the group, or a percentage of people among the group, who are sensitive to an environment being dangerous to wellbeing, because it tells the rest of the group that eventually that will be dangerous to their wellbeing.

Bianca: Yes, exactly. And to say to others, 'This is a great environment.' The gift of attention to subtlety and nuance.

Hannah: What do you know about the relationship between the brain and the stomach? I am interested in gut instinct/intuition.

Bianca: What we've seen in brain-imaging studies in highly sensitive people is that sensitivity is associated with greater activation of the insula, and the insula is involved in visceral sensations. The insula is a cortical region linked with self-awareness, interception, pain-processing and addiction. It's an essential component of the pain matrix, being involved in the assessment of nociceptive stimulus intensity. Highly sensitive people are deep-reading their environment all the time and storing it, and I think that sometimes that can result in having an intuition about something from all that information being processed deeply.

Hannah: Where do you want to take your research next?

Bianca: I would love to continue to examine the biological basis of the traits. We are in the infancy of understanding sensitivity. And I think it's important to do this research because, though there are people to whom you can show the research and it will be like talking to a stone – they just don't get it – for a lot of others, including highly sensitive people, they think, 'That describes me, I understand myself better, I can understand I am not a problem, that my traits have value and that they are a gift to myself and others.'

———————————

That was the second time Dr Bianca Acevedo had graciously agreed to be interviewed by me. I find her work fascinating. To return to the questions I asked at the start: are there those of us who feel more empathy? Yes, it would appear that those with a higher degree of sensitivity feel a greater degree of empathy. The science of it – Dr Acevedo looked at participants' brains in scanning machines and, showing participants visual images of loved ones and strangers, looked at their brains' reactions to others' displays of emotion. HSPs showed greater empathy and, in addition, greater planning of behaviour, pre-thought and greater combining of multisensory information.

What is empathy useful for? Prior to really understanding Dr Acevedo's research, I had not fully grasped the meaning of empathy in relation to HSPs. I now feel more illuminated, understanding that empathy is a characteristic of many of us, but particularly of HSPs. That its function is appropriate response. It took me a while to let the meaning of appropriate response settle. I could not quite get excited about that language, so

I spent some time unpacking it. Appropriate response. First, what does it mean? I am going to try to be careful here, because this subject area overlaps with psychiatric diagnosis. As an overview, inappropriate response means not acting in line with what a situation or person requires or is expecting. Appropriate response, therefore, is acting in line with what a situation or person requires or is expecting. The implications of this in the story of sensitivity are profound. Dr Acevedo said that HSPs 'might facilitate care, cooperation, planning in the species'. And though I understand her hesitation, my gut says she has absolutely hit the nail on the head. Not that HSPs are the only intelligence type able to offer those skills, more that they are naturally particularly good at them. Appropriate response – it's not very glamorous as a story headline, is it? But the more I unpack it as a concept, the more attractive it gets. Highly sensitive people, in essence, could also be called highly responsive people. Responsive to the positive and the negative of people and environments. Noticing whether an environment they are in is harmonious or under threat. Whether people they are with are OK or not. What an amazing resource to have inbuilt in a population. Like human litmus tests – acidic, alkaline. Environmental interpersonal tuning forks. Police scent dogs. There my ideas for examples run out. Appropriate response – the ability to reflect instead of immediately judging. Observe before immediately acting. To be opportunity noticers, threat detectors. Storymakers of information. I am really interested in the relationship between the knowing of information and the telling of it – I am, after all, a writer, so it is a vain interest. My instinct says that if you notice information, you start to make patterns out of that information, you start to make it into a form. And that is where stories come from. We all come from cultures in which storytelling plays a key role. I wonder whether one of the roles for HSPs (historically and now) is exactly that – storytellers.

So the important question – what does that do to our understanding of sensitivity? I think it radically changes it. It is concrete evidence of trait difference. It offers value to sensitivity – language. However, something occurs to me that feels contradictory. It relates back to the education system and the job market – what are HSPs for? Appropriate response. But many of the systems we live in look at the natural responses of HSPs and rebuke them. As Barbara Allen said to me, a proportion of HSPs act as if they are not highly sensitive – they are actively denying their own natures. This is strange maths. Entirely uneconomic. Possibly even wasteful.

Dr Bianca Acevedo has discovered that HSP brains are activating in an area responsible for pre-planning behaviour. What are the advantages of planning behaviour before you behave it? It is considered, it is likely to be more appropriate. That is a really good building block for the story of sensitivity. Those who are at the higher end of the sensitivity scale, or who are practised in the skill of sensitivity, are more likely to have considered behaviour appropriate to situation. That is useful, right? To all of us.

As a society we need a whole lot more of that. People reacting appropriately and then acting appropriately. Because it feels like big government is going in for string after string of inappropriate behaviours, inaction, poor responses. Reacting is the first step to responding, responding is doing, a considered response is most likely to be successful. It makes me think about the frequent accusation that the younger generation are snowflakes. If we reframe that a bit – does it really mean we are living in a time of ultra-reactive people? Because though I can understand why some people would think that was a negative, it is in fact a huge positive. A reactive society is one that can move to meet its own needs. That has an appropriate response to its environment. So when people say snowflake, do they in fact mean we are in a dangerous land, and we have a generation who are reacting to that? I think quite possibly so.

Finally, what is empathy for? Empathy strengthens a range of human skills, including collaboration, negotiation, emotional connection, creativity and awareness of nonverbal communication. Nonverbal communication is interesting to dig into – there are different types. Kinesics – how we move our body. Haptics – how we physically touch others. Proxemics – how we take up space. Territory – how we display power or lack of. Environment – how we present our space and ourselves. Vocalics – how we speak; volume, rhythm, tone. Chronemics – how we use our time. Attraction – how we draw attention to ourselves. Olfactics – how we use our sense of smell. And we each have preferences, which aspects we most notice about others. I believe HSPs are super-aware of all these things, and it makes me really wonder if HSPs can know things others do not. What benefit is there in being super-aware of nonverbal communication, of emotional need and connection? It connects us. It makes us more than we are on our own. It makes communities. It makes greater things possible. It makes us more than the sum of our parts.

So, how does this change sensitivity's story? Well, very simply, it gives us some more narrative. HSPs are good at empathy. Empathy is social glue. We need social glue. Also, HSP brains pre-plan behaviour – we need pre-planned behaviour. We live in a culture that is too fast on the front foot of action, often putting feet in the wrong places.

I have begun to think differently about my daughter holding back from participating at playgroup. My little daughter, circling the room, watching. I need not worry. She isn't shy, she isn't cautious – she is noticing how people are moving their bodies, how they are touching, how individuals are taking up space, who is displaying power or drawing attention to themselves and who is not. She is considering how to present in the environment, she is listening to the tone and rhythm of how people are speaking, she is noticing the smell of the room. What she is doing is valuable. She knows how to sense and read and consider her response, she knows how to tie information together. And I am becoming proud of this aspect of her character and, since she comes half from me, I guess that means I must for the first time feel proud of that aspect of myself too.

8. Gut instinct

Following on from Dr Bianca Acevedo's discovery that empathy is a key component of sensitivity in the brain, I am keen to know if there are other areas of the body that can teach us something about sensitivity and its story. Nearly all of us will have heard the phrase 'gut instinct'. We use it to describe an instinctive feeling instead of a fact-based feeling. It is also known as intuition – the ability to accumulate information without conscious reasoning. It is a feeling I have a lot, and one that I have learned to associate and understand as a component of high sensitivity, but I don't know if that is true. I imagine lots of you have felt intuition often, but just in case you haven't, it is a sudden, precise, bodily based feeling that stops you in your tracks, makes you look up from whatever else you might be doing and listen. It feels familiar and eerie at the same time. It has been described as a sudden mysterious impulse towards a particular decision, a response to immediate environment and sometimes a sort of throwing forwards into the future.

One of the reasons I want to explore the connection between intuition and sensitivity is that fortune-tellers used to be called 'sensitives', the idea being that they were using their sensitivity to read, sense, know, commune and connect. And not just fortune-tellers, also alternative therapists, psychics, pagans, all reportedly draw on the skill of sensitivity to connect to other energies. I don't know how I feel about this, I don't know what I believe. One of the reasons I am hesitant is that I got totally freaked out by a psychic when I was a young teenager. I was accompanying my mum to a psychic fair after her mum had died and she was in deep grief. I was just walking around the room waiting for my mum, and one of the psychics caught me by the wrist and said, 'I am going to give you this information and don't pay me for it. When you were born you nearly died because of your shoulder, but you were pulled through to this world and because of that, you are accompanied always by a deceased member of your family, you have an angel, you will never be alone.'

She was right about the shoulder and the near death, and I was terrified. When I got home, I went straight to my teenage bedroom and thought, I am being watched all the time, I will never be alone. I became cross at the psychic for telling me what she believed. And whether she was connecting with spirits, or simply watching my posture and observing long-term structural shoulder damage, who knows? Either way she was using skills of deep noticing and reading to understand. I would argue that those skills connect strongly with the traits of HSPs. I am not saying all psychics, alternative therapists and so forth are HSPs – I bet there are thousands who are not. However, I think the skillset that these practices and professions require draws on the skills of sensitivity, and as such I would posit that there are a higher than average number of HSPs.

It's a long-standing joke in my family that we are a family of witches, that we can read people's minds and we will often know what is about to happen and what is needed. Often, when we've expressed what we thought was going to happen and then it happens, others ask us, 'How did you know?' We don't know how we know, but it is uncanny. My mum will say things like 'Don't trust that person' or 'This is what is going to happen' and despite all visible evidence, she will always, and I mean *always*, be right. We know who is going to call before they call, we will often have been deeply thinking about them for a time before the call. We know innately how to fix things, people, with natural remedies, how to create soothing spaces, the movement and names of things in our natural environment, we know the deep history of those around us, we tell a lot of stories, talk about what we notice, and we make places for people to gather. Often people in danger or need present themselves in our lives.

My mum often has things happen to her such as – in the course of one week – she found an electrician hanging unconscious from a harness up a telegraph wire, she screeched to a halt to avoid running over an alcohol-poisoned thirteen-year-old, and a man had a heart attack right outside her office door. She intervened in every instance and assisted. And that is not an unusual week for her. Strangers talk to us on the street; often we are privileged to be told whole life stories. We joke we would have been burned at the stake had we lived a few hundred years ago – and although it's a joke, we are in some way also being serious. What we are talking about really is our sensitivity, drawing on the skill of our intuition or gut instinct. I want to know, does intuition have any relationship to sensitivity? Is there any scientific evidence? Is it quite literally connected to the gut? Is intuition even real?

As a place to begin, I asked Dr Elaine Aron, 'What do you believe the relationship is between intuition and HSPs?' and she responded with, 'I can't speak from a research point of view, because it's very hard to define and measure intuition. I think of it as knowing things without knowing how you know them, and certainly if you process things deeply, not all of it is processed consciously. But intuition or decisions may arise from what seems like nowhere. So yes, it's hard to see how intuition could not be related to high sensitivity.' To begin to investigate this I wanted to talk first to a gut specialist – to understand how the gut works in response to the brain and feelings. Meet Professor Nick Spencer at Flinders University in Australia. We arranged to speak at an early-in-the-morning time for me and early-in-the-evening time for him and logged into Zoom at our opposite ends of the day and night.

Nick: Hi, my name is Professor Nick Spencer. I work as a researcher at Flinders University in Australia. My work focuses on the gut–brain axis. I am interested in developing techniques that have been previously unavailable to the field to address major questions that have eluded scientific investigation.

Research in my laboratory is primarily directed to understanding the neurophysiological basis of pain pathways in visceral organs, and the neural control mechanisms that underlie control of the gut-to-brain axis.

Hannah: Nick, I am so delighted to talk to you, thank you for your time.

Nick: Well, I'm flattered that you decided to get in touch!

Hannah: That is funny, every researcher I've spoken to has said something similar. Does that come from a kind of research modesty?

Nick: No, I think it's something else – fear of not being believed in your research by the external scientific community. For example, we just ran this conference, and I managed to get the only Nobel Prize-winner doing work on the gut to be a speaker. I was fortunate enough to spend the week with him and discovered that, for the vast majority of his research career, nobody believed a word of what he said. He believed that bacteria lived in the stomach. But everybody thought the stomach was too acidic and no bacteria could live in such an environment. But he believed in his work, never gave up, and funded all his research himself. It took years of persistence, but many years after he published his findings he proved that bacteria do reside in the stomach and can cause stomach ulcers, potentially leading to stomach cancers. His tenacity saved the lives of millions of people, as they can now treat the bacteria in the stomach. This, of course, is Professor Robin Warren, originally from Adelaide. He never got a penny of federal funding.

Hannah: I suppose that shows that sometimes if you know something to be right, you have to find a way to ignore the voices of those around you. Nick, I am really interested in the gut and intuition. I don't understand how the brain and the stomach work in relation to each other. Can you tell me a little about that, please?

Nick: Yes, to give you a little context – there is very, very little known about the gut. Until recently, the gut wasn't really as favourable an organ to research and wasn't really taken as seriously as, for example, the brain or the heart. In fact, when I did my PhD twenty-three years ago, there was comparatively little research into the gut, so gut–brain research is a relatively new frontier. Now the field of gut–brain communication is absolutely electric. Large numbers of new and established laboratories are now turning their attention to how signals arising from the gut can modulate brain activity. What is clear is that the gut is complex, poorly understood and under-researched, despite being the largest organ in the abdomen.

The first important thing to know is that the gut has its own brain, so to speak. It is unlike any other organ in that it has its own completely independent nervous system, called the enteric nervous system, which can operate completely independently of brain and spinal cord. In 1992, I was an undergraduate student doing a science degree and we had a practical that involved studying a segment of mouse colon. I was astonished and mesmerized by the fact that, even though the colon was isolated from the animal, every two to three minutes there was a contraction of the muscle that propelled content, like a tube of toothpaste. And I thought, how is it doing this? How are the muscles contracting and relaxing? And what is the mysterious 'clock' or 'pacemaker' responsible?

Then we were given anaesthetics to apply to the segment of isolated colon, and all these contractions stopped. So, what this showed us was that the enteric nervous system was essential for generating contractions along the colon. I was fascinated, and developed an insatiable desire to understand more about how the gut nervous system worked.

Now we believe the enteric nervous system in the gut wall is actually the 'first brain', because it evolved before the brain in our skulls. The best evidence of this is one of the first organisms to develop on earth, known as a Hydra, which is much like a tube, with a mouth and an anus, that contracts and relaxes with its intrinsic nervous system. It has no conscious or sophisticated brain like us. Hydra still exist today! So we believe the enteric nervous system in humans formed before the central nervous system (our brain in our head).

So now we have two main systems for reading information, and there are lots of connections between the two. The question then is, how does the gut brain talk to the big brain? We know that good regulation requires the brain and the stomach to be in constant good communication. But what I find interesting is that if you disconnect the gut from the brain, the gut keeps working as its own brain.

Hannah: And so, the gut is really the body's first control system?

Nick: Yeah, absolutely. And so, your question I think is, how do the brain and the gut work together?

Hannah: Yes, I think that human beings have a long history of saying things like I just knew, or my gut told me. But somehow there's this feeling in the body, which is not necessarily a heart feeling and does not feel purely like a brain feeling. It feels rooted deeper in the body, and it feels so true, so where is the research for that?

Nick: Colloquially people use phrases such as I had a gut feeling that, you know, the train was coming, which have absolutely no scientific basis. What is very real is feeling a stress response to a situation and that having an impact on your gut. And there's strong evidence that if you experience early-life stress, years after that stress you can have a hypersensitive gut.

A sort of gut memory. A supersensitive gut that remembers the sensory nerves and experiences.

So, there are two major pathways connecting the gut to the brain. If you think of the spinal cord, right, think if someone broke their back and couldn't feel anything. Right. People think of the spinal cord, the spinal pathways, as being just for pain, but they're doing far more than that, they are communicating all the time. Remove them and, for example, you would drink twice as much water and become unwell.

Hannah: So, are they always sending messages to each other?

Nick: Absolutely. There are sensory nerves that send signals from the gut to the brain, and motor nerves that send signals from the brain to the gut. They are constantly active.

OK, so say you are meeting someone new, and you know, you've got this strange feeling, it could be a combination or interplay of both. Nerve communication between the gut and brain is never silent. There's always activity in these pathways. How much activity there is in these pathways determines how we 'feel'.

In essence, the question I don't think anyone has a good answer to is, what is the mechanism that could physiologically explain the feeling of gut instinct, what's the pathway underlying that? Is it sensory? Or is it motor, or a combination of both? Probably a combination of both.

This area of thinking is an extremely fertile field, which is poorly understood. So, you know, in your book, it's not about writing about no, that gut instinct does not exist, it's that we do not know enough yet.

Hannah: Do you think anyone will ever be able to prove intuition or gut instinct?

Nick: It's a good question. It's hard to know, isn't it? Because that's how science works, you don't know that the thing is possible until it's possible.

I think it is interesting that a cohort can predict an occurrence. For example, do you remember the Indian Ocean earthquake and tsunami in 2004? All the animals had moved up the hills before the water hit. Now, is that a gut instinct that they knew that that was coming?

I'm thrilled you're doing this and I commend you, because a lot of scientists couldn't do what you're doing, because of the fear of professional ridicule. But there might be something in it, who knows? We need other types of information distributors like you, to put out seemingly weird theories, because often that is how people start to research them seriously.

It is clear from talking to Professor Spencer that the gut is not a popular research field, and that feels like a shame, but clearly he and others are doing important work to move that along. Despite that, there are some discoveries here: the gut has its own brain, is independent and interconnected. The gut is older than the brain and is mutually in charge of us. This is a more embodied understanding in a specific place, the gut. This contradicts the dominant view we hold in the West that the brain is the place of decisions and feelings. The gut is, along with our brain, always scanning our environment and interpersonal communications, taking in information (literally and abstractly) and responding. I find it interesting that our body is doing such active, rooted work constantly. Of course it is – we are, after all, a body moving through and experiencing the world. I think many of us just forget our body as a place of experience and prioritize our brain and its thoughts, reactions, and feelings. I know I do.

I am, however, no closer to knowing whether the gut can tell us anything about intuition and sensitivity. I am struck by what Professor Spencer said about the researcher who studied bacteria in the gut, and no one believed him, but he turned out to be correct. What conviction that must have required, to stay the course when others doubted. And I cannot help but wonder whether intuition will prove to be one of those areas of research that in the future is proven. But even as I type that I can hear how like an alien aircraft believer that sounds. I am left with the words 'We don't know until we know' ringing in my ear.

I thought long and hard about where to go next in this investigation, and remembered that my therapist often references intuition, and that she uses it not as a hypothetical thing but as a real thing. So, I wondered if psychology may hold a different understanding of gut instinct and intuition. It was clear to me that if I was going to find someone who knew about this subject area, it was going to be emerging current research. I knew I wanted to speak to someone whose work sits exactly in the research field between the brain and the body. A lot of possible leads led to dead ends, but finally the head of the board for Cambridge Junction (an arts venue), Nicola Buckley, who is also the Associate Director for the Centre for Science and Policy at the University of Cambridge, suggested I talk to Professor Simone Schnall.

Simone: My name is Simone Schnall, and I am a professor of experimental social psychology at the University of Cambridge, in the Department of Psychology. I direct a research group called the Mind, Body and Behaviour Laboratory.

Hannah: Your research explores the interaction between thoughts and feelings and the body. I am interested in the relationship between the mind, feelings and the gut – can you tell me anything about that?

Simone: The gut is quite a central part of my work, how very basic feelings that we experience as if they're happening in the gut can influence thought processes and behaviour. For example, morality helps people decide between right and wrong. Typically, one assumes, of course, that people are only guided by rational consideration and then decide that somebody did something bad. But we're proposing that alongside rational thought, there are basic feelings, intuitions, and that they colour our decisions. We propose that this evolutionarily basic feeling feeds into morality because it's very similar to situations where if we come across food that smells bad, we're not going to eat it; if we see a surface that looks dirty and sticky, we don't want to touch it; we don't want to be exposed to people coughing at us or showing other signs that they carry a contagious disease. The role of disgust is to protect us. We suggest that that is the most basic function of disgust, and that it can also be applied to the social realm. So, when we come across people who could harm us, we have that same feeling of disgust and we feel repulsed, because it's an indication that this is a bad situation, this could be problematic for you, and in an extreme case, it could even kill you. Once you experience one type of threat, you cannot afford to expose yourself to even more risk.

Hannah: So, it's kind of like an activated alarm system?

Simone: Yes, that's exactly what it is. And there are two different things in that, that are often misunderstood as the same thing. I will try to explain our understanding of them. So firstly, we intuitively sense danger. For example, you might be walking in the woods and sense that somebody might be standing behind you, ready to hit you over the head. Or it might be some twigs falling. That is an instinct, a reflex. To turn around is so easy and cheap relatively, compared to the costly alternative. That is called intuition. And it is real. The one that is questionable is when people say things like, 'I had a feeling that if I got on that bus something might happen, so I waited for the next one.' We explain that as storytelling.

Let's say something did happen to that bus, but one would only remember if there had been really some sort of meaningful experience tied to it. But there might have been another hundred times that same thought crossed someone's mind – I have a bad feeling – but nothing happened and so the occurrence was not remembered. In hindsight, it's easy to put things together. We often do that; we all have a so-called 'psychological immune system,' which describes the idea that some people are better than others at coping with adversity and putting things in a more positive light. For example, something bad happens to them and they think, that made me a better person or offered new opportunities. It's a kind of talent. Human beings love to put together a nice life story about what was meant to be. We basically try to talk ourselves into stories where we tell ourselves that this is life unfolding as it should.

Hannah: So, it's a self-beneficial story?

Simone: Yes, in a way. We all have these self-serving biases, ways of telling ourselves we did the right thing, for example, by not going on that bus when you had a bad feeling about doing so.

I think it's worth understanding that feelings originate in the body, we only feel things through the body. It's not like you have an emotion and then you have a physical feeling. The emotion is perceiving that, for example, you feel afraid. If we're thinking back to the woods, your palms may be starting to get sweaty, you might feel your heart racing, you might feel an impulse to run away, all these bodily sensations and feelings. And then you realize you are feeling afraid and you choose an appropriate behaviour.

Dr Schnall and I talked for hours, but I think what she hits on here really gets to the heart of what I wanted to learn. So, two things are often conflated. Intuition, as in danger is behind me right now, is absolutely considered real in psychology. But 'I didn't get on that bus because I knew something was going to happen' is not. The latter is a form of storytelling, affective forecasting, the spreading apart of alternatives and an attempt at keeping the psychological immune system healthy. I suppose that makes it an act of resilience. And that is interesting, isn't it? I would argue that HSPs are more likely to use this form of self-storytelling and are in greater need of maintaining a healthy psychological immune system due to their precarious position in the world.

To link back to something Dr Bianca Acevedo said in the last chapter, HSP brains show 'activation in areas that are important for integration of information for various sensory modalities, as well as in pre-motor areas that are involved in the planning of behaviour'. To connect Professor Nick Spencer's gut research to that, the gut is the body's second brain – not lesser brain, second. I would be surprised if in due course it is not found that the gut of HSPs shows more activation in response to information, and in areas related to anticipating behaviour. Dr Simone Schnall described the gut as having an influence on behaviour in the form of herding our moral responses: for instance, disgust. Basically, the gut is gathering information to help us make appropriate decisions to keep us safe. I know it is obvious, but it has not occurred to me before that the body and brain exist in this sort of reaction chain that works at great speed – bodily sensing, emotional feeling, appropriate reaction. It makes me wonder if sometimes a bodily sensing is first felt in the gut, then our gut and brain communicate about the situation and draw information down from deep storage, but we are not doing that consciously, and so the associated feeling that arrives is one that feels off somehow. I wonder if that is what the feelings of intuition and gut instinct are. A misfiring of communication that does not link up, stomach gathering information and responding, brain not in sync.

Personally, I can live with intuition not being scientifically proven beyond sensing immediate danger. I can live with that not being witchy or magic, but instead a smart act of human endeavour to make sense of the world. I was fully prepared for the next time the witch conversation came up in my family to offer, well, it's storytelling, really, an attempt at good mental health. But I kept thinking through the multiple moments of strong intuitive feeling that I have experienced in my life and how they felt like so much more than storytelling – they felt so powerful, so outside of my normal experience. Perhaps that is just my ego not accepting that this is not real. I think of my daughter aged three, walking up to me in the kitchen, placing her hand on my stomach and saying, you have a baby in there. Me laughing, saying, no, I have not. So, I took a test, and sure enough I was pregnant, despite not showing. I think of the day my littlest sister was in a horrific car crash and then in a coma and brain-damaged – I had stopped stock-still doing my Christmas shopping, filled with the horror of knowing that something bad had happened, but with no explanation in my immediate environment, calling my dad straight away. I think of the morning I woke up knowing my best mate was pregnant, and then her calling and her saying, 'How did you know?'

I think of the day I rearranged my room in a student house, moving all my possessions to the other side of the room, and then the ceiling came down right where the bed had been. I think of the day I was in the garden hanging up washing and just knew something was wrong with my husband. I called him to find out he was having trouble with his heart and was being rushed to hospital. I think of the day my sister saw my husband's father, who complained of a bad back, and she turned to me and said, 'I know it's cancer.' The doctors said no, it's not, but had missed the diagnosis. He died a year later. I think of the time my grandad, who was a twin, had woken up in the middle of the night with a feeling of panic and dread and called his twin living in Portugal to find out that he had been in an earthquake and his house had collapsed.

These things may not have scientific evidence, but they are real in a different way. They are real in the experience of the human living them, in the way that you cannot deny a human's experience as real. That grip of the gut, that telling, listening, understanding things that we cannot possibly know. Yeah, sure, maybe I am creating narratives for myself to live in. I can only offer you my absolute honesty when I say that that primal feeling, so very deeply rooted in the gut, feels alarmingly real.

***

I did not feel much like continuing with investigating gut instinct and intuition. It felt like a dead end, being willed on only by my bloody-mindedness. But I decided to give it one more try. I was at home in the kitchen, complaining to my husband how far and wide I had researched and not succeeded, and he said, 'Have you tried googling it?' I laughed and said, 'No, you don't google research, it's lazy.' The next day at the office, I thought, OK, sure, why not?, so I typed into the search bar 'Are gut instinct and/or intuition real?' I laughed when the results flipped up. A massive recent raft of articles and social media alerts. Professor Joel Pearson at the Future Minds Lab, NHMRC fellow, MindX. The social media posts said things like 'the science of intuition' and 'sixth sense provable'. Joel Pearson's research takes the idea that most people accept the idea of intuition, but that science currently does not. He and fellow researchers Galang Lufityanto and Chris Donkin conducted a study in 2016 to examine the existence of intuition, which they defined as 'the ability to make successful decisions without rational, analytical thought or inference'.

This is a description of the study. Participants were asked to predict which direction a dot on a computer screen might move. While this was happening, they viewed flash imagery of the direction the dots were going to move next, meaning the images didn't register consciously, because they were moving so fast. But the participants were absorbing them intuitively, they were still seeing them. They were then asked again to predict the direction of the dots. The question was, would the participants use this intuitive information to help decide the direction of the dots?

Could the brain accurately predict their direction? The answer is yes. Amanda Hooten explained, in an article in the *Sydney Morning Herald*, that a real-life example might read like this:

> In the real world, we can see how this experiment helps explain intuition. Say we enter a restaurant we've never visited before. Without our conscious awareness, our brain processes a raft of information: the floor is dirty, the flowers are fake, there's a smell. Instantly, it correlates that information to previous experiences in restaurants: dirty floor plus fake flowers plus weird smell equals bad eating experience. We don't consciously perceive any of this, just as experiment subjects didn't perceive the emotional images. All we perceive is a sudden, strong intuition: no, we should not eat here.

Professor Joel Pearson's research shows us that intuition is fast and physical. Intuitive judgements use the amygdala, an ancient, instantaneous, flight-or-fight system of our brain. It's no accident therefore that an alternative name for intuition is 'gut feeling.' We feel sick, our heart rate rises, we sweat or our gut responds quite literally.

This research, though new and in its early stages, does appear to show that intuition in terms of the body reading the environment, the gut reading the environment on a subconscious level, is real and that we are also capable of predicting how something will turn out. This experiment characterizes the qualities of intuition, fast and physical, and shows that it is subconscious information stored in the brain and body, that some information is read consciously and some subconsciously. I wonder if it is also possible that this experiment shows that sometimes the brain and the body are listening at different response times. If you can know something in your gut, but your brain has not caught up yet.

In terms of HSPs and this skill, I refer to what Dr Elaine Aron said at the start of this chapter, that although intuition is hard to quantify, it would be surprising if those who are deep-reading their environment all the time (HSPs) did not also have a strong sense of intuition. HSPs can read people well – tone, pauses, micro-expressions, body language – they are reading in a depth and to a degree that others are not. I think this connects with what Dr Bianca Acevedo said: it is all about providing appropriate response. I have begun to think of us all as a deep-storage vault system at the bottom of the sea, containing vast amounts of consciously and unconsciously absorbed information. Occasionally a shadow passes over, like something large over a portal window, and in that instant our body knows, our gut knows, but our brain lags a bit.

While I was writing the end of this chapter, a brand-new piece of information flew into my inbox. To give it context, I was having a self-doubting day. I was thinking, here I am talking on and on about sensitivity, and what if this is not something anyone else finds relevant to them, what if I am talking into a vacuum, and I could feel my distress level rising. I noticed it and thought, aha, I am going to take a break. So, I closed my laptop and walked to the shop to buy some soup and when I got back to my inbox, I had received an email from a stranger. This happens sometimes since I have started working on sensitivity. It was from an artist called Anna Falcini. She emailed me to say she makes work about atmosphere and landscape, that she had been struggling with her insomnia due to her high sensitivity and that she had happened upon my radio piece. She was getting in touch because she wanted to tell me that it had been relevant for her, and had I read the article in *The Observer* last week about intuition. No, I had not, so I went and read it. It was by David Robson, author of *The Intelligence Trap*, and it explored interoception.

Interoception sounded familiar, so I checked back in the interviews for this book and found that it was something Dr Bianca Acevedo had mentioned. Interoception here is described as a hidden sense that shapes your wellbeing. It is something we all have but are aware of to different degrees. It is your brain's awareness of your bodily state, which is transmitted from receptors in major organs. Including, wait for it...the gut! An example is: something is uncomfortable, our gut clenches, our brain observes this and connects, yes, I am feeling uncomfortable. This is one of the fastest moving areas of neuroscience. David Robson explains:

There is growing evidence that signals sent from our internal organs to the brain play a major role in regulating emotions...Much of the processing of these signals takes place below conscious awareness: you won't be aware of the automatic feedback between brain and body that helps to keep your blood pressure level, for instance, or the signals that help to stabilize your blood sugar levels. But many of these sensations – such as tension in your muscles, the clenching of your stomach, or the beating of your heart – should be available to the conscious mind, at least some of the time. And the ways you read and interpret those feelings will have important consequences for your wellbeing.

Basically, emotions begin with non-conscious bodily reactions. The body notices first. This can also be interpreted as intuition. As David Robson explains, 'This suggests that our interoception lies behind our sense of intuition, when something just feels "right" or "wrong" without us being able to explain why.'

I think this article and research bring together in an important way things that Simone Schnall, Nick Spencer and Joel Pearson all touch on. If you are someone who for whatever reason ignores the conversation your body is having with your brain, it can have real impact on your wellbeing. Research, as I said, is going on apace, and I would bet all I have that in the not-too-distant future, they will start to research intuition and different types of people. I have a strong instinct that they will find that HSPs are more aware of the conversation between their body and their brain. They will find that those who are more sensitive are more aware of intuition and its shaping of our decision-making. Time will tell.

In the meantime, as the parent of a highly sensitive child with a strong sense of intuition, I know the certainty of the look on my daughter's face when she tells me, 'I feel like something is going to happen, I can feel it here, in my tummy.' I have tried saying, 'Are you worried about something?', 'Are you feeling unwell?', trying to identify something in the environment or in her psychology that might be causing this. She shakes her head bluntly side to side, a little annoyed, annoyed at me for not understanding. The thing is, I really understand. Lots of us do. So, I am not going to tell her that it isn't real. I am going to hold an open mind, listen to what she tells me, listen to the way she is reading the world.

What does this do to the story of sensitivity? There are wide-ranging narrative reports of highly sensitive people being highly intuitive. It is scientifically accepted that gut instinct is a real thing in terms of your gut reading danger in a situation. There is emerging research that suggests evidence for intuition. But there is still much we cannot explain, yet. The research shows us that the body notices first, that there are systems working in and on us below our level of conscious awareness, continuously. I wonder if HSPs are slightly more aware of these non-conscious bodily reactions. I wonder if they are listening slightly differently – I mean, they are listening differently to nearly every other variable, is it such a stretch to apply that inwards to the bodily response also? I find it reassuring to think that in each of us, in each major organ, there are receptors, picking up and reading, assessing and sorting, continuously. We are so reactive. That is so human.

9. Working it

'What do you want to be when you grow up?'

The most exhaustively asked question of our young. What do you want to be? Depends on who you are, what your skillset is, and your privilege. We have strong ideas as a culture about what constitutes success. Can you afford to buy a house? Do you have nice things? Can you afford nice holidays? What is your pension looking like? These are presented to us as a) normal b) success. We live in a sum: productivity + net worth = your value. What is each of us worth? We are worth what we are in relation to the job economy.

We measure value based on economic productivity. To see evidence of this, you only need look at the fact that society does not value all professions equally, or even closely, and by value I mean we have vastly different scales of financial reward. Sectors such as science and finance have exceptionally high salaries. Education, care, heritage and the arts have exceptionally low salaries. Those who are high on the sensitivity scale are most likely to be drawn to careers in the latter.

Is it time we reconsidered the contribution and value to society of different professions? This has happened naturally over the last decade at a few key historical moments, such as the banking crisis: people suddenly realized that bankers are paid vast salaries, and started to ask why, as tons of bankers still, despite the crisis, got huge bonuses and pay-outs. There is nothing wrong with bankers, we need them, just as we need every sector of employment that exists, pretty much. But bankers are not the be-all and end-all of human success, and we need to really think about what we mean when we talk about value, because it has huge implications for the type of society we live in. So, what do we mean by value? And how do we treat sensitivity in relation to the world of work?

As Ellis Lawlor, Helen Kersley and Susan Steed explained in their joint article published by the New Economics Foundation:

> Pay matters. How much you earn can determine your lifestyle, where you can afford to live, and your aspirations and status. But to what extent does what we get paid confer 'worth'? Beyond a narrow notion of productivity, what impact does our work have on the rest of society, and do the financial rewards we receive correspond to this? Do those that get more contribute more to society?

There is a difference between the social contribution of your job and the value inherent in that versus the financial contribution of your job and the value inherent in that. To go beyond what people are paid and to understand value in broader terms is incredibly useful; it gives us a much more rounded perspective of the world we live in. The article includes examples comparing the contribution of different types of jobs. Here I include three as an illustration.

Childcare workers

What they do – care for our young children pre school.

Our understanding of their value – low respect, low pay.

In reality – As Lawlor, Kersley and Steed point out, for every £1 they are paid, childcare workers generate between £7 and £9.50 worth of benefits to society. Childcare workers release earning potential for families by allowing parents to keep working.

Bankers

What they do – supposedly make money for the economy.

Our understanding of their value – high value, high respect, high pay.

Salaries often range between £500,000 and £10 million.

In reality – they brought the global financial system to brink of collapse and, according to the New Economic Foundation article, cost £7 of social value for £1 of value generated.

Hospital cleaners

What they do – maintain hygiene standards, ensuring patients get better quicker and that the hospital environment does its job.

Our understanding of their value – not high: often on zero-hour contracts, very low pay, low respect.

In reality – huge contribution to societal wellbeing. Again, from the above source, for every £1 they are paid, £10 in social value is gained.

We equate net worth and productivity with social and self-worth. Great for some, dangerous for many. Our economic system is in danger of ignoring the aspects of humanity that matter the most, those things being empathy, care, education, cooperation and so forth. Reward and value are dramatically out of alignment, and our value system, education and politics have allowed that to happen. What that means is that people with traits such as sensitivity, who are drawn to sectors that are low paid but have sensitivity at their centre, have radically different understandings about society's view of their skills. We each may individually and internally within sectors hold self-worth in relation to our work. For example, as an artist and educator, I take great nourishment and self-value from knowing that, though I am in a sector that is not well paid, the work I do engages people who might otherwise not be engaged. That is what keeps me going, when yearly I struggle to get by and pay my tax bill and when the government does not support freelancers in my sector during a global crisis. I do this job for selfish reasons. I am doing it because it suits my skills, I am motivated by the meaning of the work, I am good at it and I also think it offers something to society. But it's hard to keep telling yourself that story when society tells you that your job is of low value and cuts the educational routes that lead to it.

Who do we say has value? And what do we mean by contribution? My Grandma Joan was a cleaner at Cambridge University for over forty-five years. She is ninety-four. She has lived an extraordinary life. If you ask her, she will say she has 'not done much, she was just a cleaner and raised three sons'. Being a cleaner is not a job associated with high success and societal contribution. She has always struggled financially, but she has always been generous with her money. She has always worked hard, but she has always been poorly paid.

That set of variables does not sit easily with me. I know the reality of the work she did, cleaning rooms. But what about the human worth of the work she did working at an internationally excellent university with students from around the world? I know she got to know a lot of the students whose rooms she cleaned.

I know she learned their names, taught some of them better spoken English, drew maps for them about where to find resources in the city, she even spent time finding specific things some of them needed. She met people from all around the world, away from home and their communities, and she gave them a safe contact point, a welcome navigation. She was paid a very low salary; she has a low view of her contribution. I think, though, that what she contributed was helping international students to feel safe and welcome in another country. What that does is increase good relationships between countries, allow the spread of people and ideas across geographical boundaries. I think that is important, but she cannot hear me when I say that, so entrenched are her ideas of value against the system of bigger, better, more.

The world of work is in a big process of change. There is much we do not know about the future; we don't know what the jobs of the future will be, for example. But we do know that technology is playing an increasing role in the workplace. In fact, in quite a lot of cases, technology is replacing the skills of workers. So surely the one sector in which sensitivity is not useful is the tech industry. Meet Chris Thompson.

———————————

Chris: I'm Chris Thompson. I've been in IT for the past twenty-five years in both the public and private sectors. In that time, I've supported several successful high-profile projects, including the redevelopment of several critical digital services across policing, education and defence. I now lead the solutions architecture team for the lingerie company Bravissimo.

Hannah: Chris, you and I have met previously, you were in the audience of a festival where I did a talk about sensitivity. And you stayed behind afterwards to tell me that as an employer you're very interested in sensitivity.

Chris: Yes. New technology advances are now much more focused on the user experience. And one of the things we're finding is that when you're developing new software, it needs to be much more focused on how people are going to react, how they are going to interact with those systems. We call this the user experience 'UX', and what is important is how the user emotionally responds to the software. Because we need to design software that makes people feel satisfied, there is an increasing desire for people who can sit with software developers when they are trialling that software, to see how they are reacting to it, so that we can make changes to the software to make it more user-friendly.

Hannah: So, depending on how the user feels about the interface, it may be successful or not?

Chris: Yes, absolutely. And highly sensitive people are the key to that, they are the ones who are most likely to notice if the software is not satisfying.

We want software that is intuitive and responds to what the user is trying to do. And in the testing phase of a piece of software, you need some good skills in people who can notice and respond to how users doing the testing are responding. You need people who can ask questions and read people. It is a special set of skills, people who notice and read people. Traditionally, technology has been very focused on people with technical skills. This is much more about those with a more emotional understanding of how people react to the software. Someone once said to me, no one has written a user instruction book for Facebook, people just know how to use Facebook.

Hannah: The relationship between technology and the skill of sensitivity is an interesting one. What do you think of the commonly held idea that emotional sensitivity is one of the key fundamental differences between us and technology?

Chris: I think that user interaction will become more and more important as time progresses and the digital permeates our lives. It is going to become very important that technology moves with and is tailored to our language, our mood.

Hannah: So highly sensitive people might potentially be people to look to employ in an increasingly competitive market?

Chris: Yes, I have several people on my team who are what we call UX specialists. I look to recruit people who are very emotionally aware and intuitive on that team. They don't need a lot of technical skill, but they do need to know how to test an interface in front of an individual to see how they respond to it.

Hannah: What skills are the UX specialists using when they are working to make the tech more intuitive?

Chris: They are listening. Picking up on body language. Engaging with the user in a way that says if it's not working for you, what would you expect to see? It's not a technological language, it's a human-based language. And so, when you're recruiting you are looking for people who combine tech skills with some sort of sensitivity skills.

Hannah: It seems like one of the things that technology has been based on in the past is 'What does somebody think?' And now it's moving towards 'What do they feel?' Is that a fair assessment?

Chris: Yes, it's called 'outside-in' thinking. We start with the person and then build the software around the person. Rather than, 'Here's the software, how do I cram it into what that person needs to do?' That's certainly why a lot of government websites look better than they used to and are much more focused around what you're trying to do rather than what somebody else thinks you're trying to do.

Hannah: So, do you believe that a product could fail because it isn't designed with enough of the user experience in mind?

Chris: Yes, absolutely. A large reason for IT project failure isn't because of functionality gaps; it does everything it needs to do, but the users do not respond to it and do not want to embed it into their work life.

What interests me about what Chris Thompson has shared is that sensitivity and technology seemed to be odd playmates but, in fact, for technology to do what we need it to do now, which is to be intuitive in use, we need to harness the skill of sensitivity. Skills such as noticing and reading body language, active listening and questioning are clear, concrete examples of value in a specialist and developing economy, showing that there is a place for sensitivity in what we know of future economies.

There are many professions currently where the skills of sensitivity are essential. While I was writing this, Nazir Afzal OBE was interviewed on the BBC radio programme *Desert Island Discs*. He is a British solicitor with experience in the legal areas of child sexual exploitation and violence against women. He is a practising Muslim, with outspoken views in favour of women's rights and against forced marriage, female genital mutilation and honour killings.

> You are not trained in law school to be sensitive,
> to show empathy, to demonstrate humanity, even.
> Hopefully you've got it, but it's essential that you
> can listen, are able to understand. You never really
> understand a person until you can put yourself in
> their shoes, inside their skin and walk around in it,
> and I have always wanted to do that. And I have cried
> a lot during my legal career, because these people have
> been touched by real pain, but at the same time, I get
> tremendous satisfaction in giving them something
> that they probably lacked before, which is justice.

This is a rare set of beliefs to hear from someone in a position of power, pay and esteem. Nazir Afzal is correct: sensitivity is not taught, but there are professions where it is essential. He reminded me of this quote from Peter Levine PhD about what makes a good therapist:

> Presence, the ability to remain centred and resonate
> in a primitive way with your clients. The ability to

connect with their inner world, nervous system to nervous system. Let difficult feelings and sensations move through you, showing your client how to feel their feelings, and then let them go.

Obviously these two jobs require using the skill of sensitivity differently. I am really interested in this idea of 'nervous system to nervous system'. How to centre in on where a person is, to really hear them, to hold a space for them – an extraordinary skillset. A lot of the work that HSPs are drawn to involves working with people experiencing trauma – the police, nurses, psychiatrists, teachers, lawyers, social workers. I am curious about this tension between traumatic work, its impact and the hyper-empathy of HSPs. I wanted to speak to someone who works with people in these professions; it turns out I already knew them.

Wendy: Hi, I am Wendy Showell Nicholas, a registered counsellor and psychotherapist, NLP master practitioner, coach, independent social worker, author, mindfulness teacher, educator and speaker. All of my work is research-informed. I believe that wellbeing should be prioritized in all areas of our work and life. Certainly, trauma recovery and healing from difficult life events should not be faced alone. In addition to being extremely helpful for people who have experienced or work with trauma, I believe that therapy is for everyone. It should be a normal life experience to build and maintain general wellbeing, just like going to a GP, the gym or a spa!

I am a proud Yorkshire woman whose four children and one grandchild challenge me to practise what I preach in very busy circumstances!

Hannah: We met at a festival called The Good Life Experience, where I was giving a talk about sensitivity. You were in the audience. In the talk I made the case that sensitivity was more useful than we understood it to be. After the talk there was a Q&A and a gentleman in the audience put his hand up and said that he did not think sensitivity could possibly be useful. He even asked the audience to do a poll on whether they agreed. It was quite an amazing moment. He got a little cross that the audience did not agree with him. And you very graciously stepped in and diverted the conversation and explained that you work with a lot of HSPs and that it need not mean an inability to cope with life.

Wendy: Yes, I think he equated sensitivity with weakness. And he equated it with a lack of resilience. I don't think he could really hear what you were saying.

Hannah: It was a fascinating moment. It kind of live illustrated exactly the challenge I was talking about. But Wendy, could you tell me a little about the nature of your work, please?

Wendy: Sure. I work with a wide range of people and organizations, including the NHS, the police, social workers, doctors, nurses. HSPs are attracted to those jobs because their skillset really matches the job, and because they have a high level of empathetic understanding. HSPs tend to process things very deeply, and often have a real passion for a cause or a subject. And that means that they can often get attracted to careers that they find meaningful, where there is good to be done in the world. So often those careers are things like social work, sometimes law, certainly medical professions, and sometimes police, teachers – professions with clear value behind them.

A lot of my work is about working with people to maintain optimum performance in their life and at work. In relation to the highly sensitive person that can be a little bit trickier. HSPs have a real wealth of skills and abilities in terms of working with people: understanding nuance, sensitivities in workplace situations.

A lot of the people I work with, the nature of their work is very taxing, for example jobs where they might be vulnerable to secondary trauma. Unfortunately, if they don't care for themselves and take a lot of recovery time, it can have an impact on their wellbeing. The point I made to the man at the festival was that there's an equation for optimum performance. And instead of burning out, which lots of people do, not just highly sensitive people, maintaining a long and productive career as an effective practitioner is possible. The formula is: maintaining high empathic concern, high emotional intelligence, but low empathic distress. That's the formula that I work to embed.

Our society fetishizes being busy and overworking, which is a problem because it usually leads to inadequate and dangerous service delivery. There is a lot of narrative about people being told to toughen up, to develop a thick skin to deal with complex situations. But I find the opposite is true. I find that a thickened skin is often a sign of burnout, ineffective emotional functioning, whereas people who function intelligently in terms of their emotions tend to maintain an ability to engage empathetically with people, to be aware of and respond to the emotional impact we have on others and vice versa.

Hannah: Wendy, can you tell me a little more about the formula. What is the difference between high empathic concern and empathic distress?

Wendy: Absolutely. High empathic concern is linked to compassion. It is the ability to have a real sense of someone else's suffering and to feel motivated to alleviate that suffering. It is a resourceful state. We feel a sense of the other person's pain and feel compassion and connection to that person in their suffering, but it is still theirs, we are not overwhelmed or dragged down by it. Emotional distress, in contrast, is where we feel compassion for the other person's pain but rather than our focus being on their suffering, we become overwhelmed. Witnessing their pain becomes a source of suffering for us. This is more likely to happen if our own resources are low. It is a less resourceful state, as our own suffering gets in the way of us being able to help the other person in their suffering. We want to avoid connecting with them emotionally because it is too painful for us.

Hannah: When you work with individuals/organizations, what's the nature of the work that you do with them?

Wendy: I run several different services. For some companies, I will run a helpline for professionals in crisis, those that have hit a brick wall in terms of capacity, especially when they're dealing with really difficult subject matter, particularly in social work and law. Alongside helplines, people can come to me for longer-term counselling; also I go into workplaces and do awareness-raising seminars about general wellbeing. I'm a real believer in not just offering emergency help, but also working to change workplace culture. Workplace cultures really feed into an unhealthy working practice now. I'm quite strict, working with people to help them realize that it is part of their professional responsibility to maintain fitness to practise. And that is about practical implemented self-care.

I think there is a huge workplace culture problem. I genuinely feel this is something that we will look back on and think of it in the same way as we think of smoking. Currently we have a culture of being expected twenty-four hours a day to be connected to our phones, we've got to be available, we've got to be thinking the job all the time, answering emails after midnight – that kind of pressure is not sustainable for people. It's everywhere, it impacts on all of us, the signs are there.

And in terms of HSPs, think of them like canaries in the coalmine. It usually impacts on them first, and more, that damage is visible in a really clear way. It is happening to all of us, but less visibly in non-HSPs. If we make things right for the highly sensitive person, then the knock-on effect benefits everybody.

Hannah: Presumably, organizations like the NHS or social services are very good at self-care and good boundaries while maintaining high empathic concern?

Wendy: Well, no, I would say no. I was thinking how I can say that delicately. Often the opposite. I'm from a social-work background, a registered social worker as well as a psychotherapist. My experience is that the caring professions are often the least good at looking after each other in their own staff. It's hard to look after yourself when your focus is outward and trying to care for people.

Hannah: What do you think organizations such as those can do to better support?

Wendy: Good question. There's something about how we work – remotely, increasingly, or hot-desking – which is unhelpful because it forces people into situations of isolation when they need to be connected. In times of change, people don't want to be hot-desking, they need to be with others who are known. So those kinds of cultural practices that are about saving money and being able to manage more 'efficiently', I think they're a false economy, because what we find is that people become less robust. Organizations need to realize that there's a lot of mileage in people having rest time. It's not about maintaining maximum output continuously; in fact, the human brain just can't function well like that, we lose creativity, problem-solving skills and emotional intelligence when we are in constant work mode. Counterintuitively, our brains need time in flow and rest state to maintain efficiency. We need to recuperate. Encouraging a culture of good work-life balance: that is what maximizes our productivity and maintains a healthy workforce.

A lot of the workplaces I have talked about, part of the nature of the work is sorrowful, seeing some of the hardest parts of being human. It is important to feel some of that sorrow, to understand it as it really is, because if you're not able to engage in some of the sorrow of your work, if you develop a 'thick skin' and don't feel anything, then you also block out joy. We can't block out feeling selectively. So, if you can't experience the sorrow, it's harder to experience the joy, and that includes the joy of your home life. And that's it. Our empathy is so important as a skill, you can't totally compartmentalize, but some boundaries are useful.

There's a cultural aspect. So, we know that in China, for example, sensitivity is seen as being valuable. There are studies of young HSP children being the most esteemed in their class. There is a theory that this difference is about awareness of taking up space and resources, the impact of each of us on our immediate environment, and the contribution of that to the economy.

The mentality we have is very Western, very American now, about bulldozing, driving forward, self-promotion. People mistake those traits for effectiveness, influence and leadership. And those things are not necessarily the same. Sometimes those traits are effective. But there are not many people who are good at knowing the worth of their peers, their employees, the team, and knowing how to bring the best out of them. And truly great leaders can take much more of an apparent backseat and facilitate their team components to be powerful.

Hannah: Do you think that it's difficult for people in the workplace to admit to their sensitivity?

Wendy: Yes. But it needn't be, I think, if someone can identify the boundaries of their own tolerance levels and practice and say, OK, I'm highly sensitive. So, when I engage in this conversation with you and say it'd be better for me if we did it in a quieter place, if the lights weren't so bright, or even if we went outside where we can get a breath of fresh air or be in green space, then I think that's an act of bravery. It shows real strength and courage. And it's brilliant role-modelling for people who maybe are not so highly sensitive and don't have those skills. It is an assertive thing to do. Being yourself and being true to who you are and just being very matter of fact about that is one of the bravest things we can do. It's easy to try to be someone else or act in a role. But being authentic, that is the opposite of weakness.

Hannah: Any advice for the HSP worker?

Wendy: Yes – HSPs can benefit from factoring in about 40 per cent more time than you think anything is going to take, because you need to account for recovery time. It's important to note this will not make you less productive. In fact, we get more done, more efficiently when we work with our tendencies rather than against them. HSPs generally have a higher recognition of their own internal processing, what's affecting them, what's not affecting them, higher than other people might have. So, my advice to anybody who thinks they are highly sensitive is be authentic, be brave, accept that you need downtime and that self-care will make you more effective in your job.

Speaking with Wendy Showell Nicholas really made me think of what is asked of those in job roles that require care. How personally taxing it must be. How tempting it must be to toughen your skin, to zone out – not out of lack of care, but out of fatigue. I think of how aware we as a population became of the value of our doctors, nurses and carers in 2020, during the pandemic. think of us all, myself included, standing on the doorstep on a Thursday evening clapping and clapping. But what are we asking of these people? We are asking them in many cases to put 'nervous system to nervous system', to use their absolute humanity as well as their other skills to do their job. That's a big ask, and I feel very humbled by those who do it. I wonder how many of them have the resources for self-care so that they are resilient resourced workers, rather than being taxed for a skill they are not properly paid for.

It's also interesting that Wendy Showell Nicholas says there is a workplace culture problem of overworking, of busyness. That is a big problem for all of us, but we are most likely to see its impact on HSPs first.

And what about jobs that do not require sensitivity as a specialist skill? A very high percentage of employment now takes place within offices. Work environments are an extension of the values of the education system – group working spaces, first hand up gets the opportunity, competition, volume and speed all prized. As such, a fair proportion of HSPs find the conditions and values of the workplace challenging. I am one of them. I always found working in an open-plan office like being in a bumper car at a fair, full of noise, collisions, busy. I used to work listening to music in headphones so that I could forget I was in an open-plan space. I was so interested in what was going on around me, noticing others, dynamics, patterns. I found team meetings tricky: so many people, the space always lacking real human connection, decision-making so fast and extroverted. Earlier in this book, Barbara Allen stated that, for an HSP, working for yourself is the ideal, setting your own boundaries and values, but that is not always possible: many careers require organizational connection and structure; lots of us simply must work for and alongside others, with people and in places that may not be the best for us but within which we need not just to survive but also to thrive.

I am freelance now and can vouch for the falling away of those concerns once I was outside an organization. Before I went freelance, though, I had the great pleasure of working with an HR consultant called Christine Garner. Christine is an internationally excellent HR specialist with great perception, and I wanted to interview her because she has worked in almost every aspect of the employment sector. Having seen her in action, I know that she is quite extraordinary – she really understands what is held to be of value in the workplace and why.

———————————

Christine: My name is Christine Garner. I've spent most of my adult working life in management and leadership, consultancy and training. And I've worked in a whole variety of organizations in the private sector, public sector, charities and lots of arts organizations and housing associations, both of which are a great passion of mine.

You and I met when I was an HR consultant with the Norfolk and Norwich Arts Festival. I worked with Jonathan Holloway, who was the Artistic Director then. We worked together on a whole variety of projects, and quite a lot of the work was about understanding people at work, understanding clients and users and how they work, and how personality and preferences come into play in the work environment.

Some people will be born with a natural, heightened awareness of what's going on around them, and what's happening with the people around them. And those people will be aware of what and how things impact on the people around them, while other people won't notice, as they'll be primarily focused on the task. You can't easily do anything about that, that's how you were born. What you can do is raise your own awareness of your natural preferences, develop an awareness of different preferences, and then work on understanding and developing the less natural skills. If you're one of the sensitive people, then you need to develop skills that will ensure your voice and viewpoint are understood. And if you are one of the people who are not so sensitive in life, then you need to develop your awareness skills.

I think if you're one of the sensitive ones, you often feel that there's upset around you, you are not heard and some people just don't understand you. And it's a bit of a mystery to you, how other people can be so clumsy. I think if you're not so sensitive, you may just not understand why people are 'so touchy', and why they 'make such a big deal out of things'. This happens in organizations everywhere. Many tend to be run in a way that doesn't support sensitive input. They look for lots of measurable evidence, they're very numbers-driven. They want 'no nonsense', they have all sorts of hard language around it, which says, 'Well, if you can't handle the heat in the kitchen, get out.' There's a lot of hard talk within organizations. And that doesn't leave a lot of space for people who are more aware of emotions, feelings, values and impact on others. So they can be left out of consultation, because they don't talk up very readily or immediately. And because of that, they're not always valued.

Part of the work I do is raising awareness throughout the organization of different types and skills, so the organization can start to develop itself, include a diversity of voices and skills. I think sensitivity as a skill in organizations is underestimated and not given much time at all.

Hannah: So, you believe it's almost treated as a sort of negative within the workplace?

Christine: Absolutely. Yeah, absolutely. I do think it's seen as a negative. But I think human beings at work are not very good at dealing with feelings and emotions. And we're awful at giving one another time to speak and time to listen.

Hannah: I agree. What do you feel a good team is made up of?

Christine: Variety, always variety. A good team is made of people with different approaches to life, different skills. The broader the spectrum of preferences and talents that a team has, the better. What that offers an organization is a team that will understand every situation and every customer from a different point of view. But the trick is, once you have that diversity, to make sure your methods include all viewpoints, to equally share, acknowledge and value a range of inputs, and not to compete but to cooperate with one another.

Hannah: I wonder what your view might be on whether highly sensitive people make good leaders.

Christine: Highly sensitive people make great leaders. The more aware a leader is of the skills and traits of themselves and others, the better a leader they are – self-awareness is very important in good leadership. We have this cultural idea that good leadership looks like someone who knows absolutely what they are going to do, tells everyone and is very clear about it. It is almost cartoonish. But that's not what good leadership is. Good leadership has breadth to it. All good leaders have both breadth and depth, their ways of interacting with people, their clients and the world in general. So sensitive people make great leaders. Insensitive people, I think, have a tougher time of being a good leader because they end up as a form of dictator, and we know what happens with that sort of leadership.

Hannah: I feel like we're headed a bit that way – dictatorship – in terms of the type of people we're putting in power.

Christine: And that's because we fall for charisma. The public love charisma. We're absolutely drawn to it. I heard charisma defined once as the ability to persuade and influence without the use of logic. And while I think it can be attractive, because it sounds certain, and it sounds as if it's all going to be simple, and all you must do is trust and follow the leader – that's not real.

I am not saying sensitive people are not charismatic, they often are, but I am saying that poor leaders sometimes try to hide behind charisma, and it is confusing *and* seductive.

Hannah: Do you feel that there's change happening within the employment sector about what skills are needed, and how workplaces are run?

Christine: Yes, I do; however, humanity does not evolve and develop at the same speed that technology does, humanity is a slower process. If you look back to the Industrial Revolution era, many workplaces were awful to work in. They're not as bad as that now, though there are new challenges. Progress and change are happening all the time. Do I think it's on the road to honouring humanity and being the best it could possibly be? Well, yeah, but it's a slow job, and there are places out there that are awful. And there are behaviours that are awful. So, I don't hold out hope that things are going to change quickly.

Hannah: Can I ask you what skills you feel sensitive people potentially have to offer the workplace?

Christine: They have an awareness of how things impact on people. And because sensitive people tune in readily and easily to the impact that things have on people, they have an amazing gift to offer. They are the ones who, if you're running an organization, will say to you, it's all very well if we do that, but I think X, Y and Z will be impacted like this. So as a leader within an organization, or as a business owner, you need to pay particular attention to them. Because those people will be right.

Hannah: Do you know of any pay scale that rewards that sensitivity as a valuable skill?

Christine: Fascinating. Um, no. I've done a lot of work around job evaluation and how to measure contribution, and I don't think sensitivity as a skill is as overtly recognized as the other things that are measurable. So pay scales tend to reward people for doing more, getting bigger, better results. And the terminology that is used within organizations is too based around measuring the hard, easily quantifiable stuff. And although I think it's the sensitivity of the sensitive people that will give you the key to selling more and selling better and developing better products and services for a wider proportion of the population, it is not recognized or measured enough, and I think that needs looking at.

Your question surprised me. And that's the value of different question types from different people. Who wouldn't want to embrace that? I don't know that it needs to be recognized in a bigger or different way to the people who are good at crunching the detail or looking at the things that are factual or evidence-based, but it's not, and it should be valued. I value your question: it just made me think completely differently.

Hannah: What do you think HSPs can do in the workplace to increase awareness and visibility of their value?

Christine: Practise things like using assertive, definite language. If you can take out the uncertainty in the language, people feel more comfortable. And understand their own value so that they can find a language to articulate it to others, particularly in performance reviews.

The work that those who are not highly sensitive can do to increase the value of HSPs in the workplace is to be curious about what it is that those other people see that they don't see. Respect and value different viewpoints, and do not make it wrong just because you don't understand it. Seriously, be curious about what is it that they see; why do they ask such a different question? Everybody must have time to speak and be listened to by everybody else. Once you hear all views, you can then take a better decision as a team or as the leader of a team. And the quality of decisions made in the workplace is dependent on the quality of the thinking that was done before the decision was taken. The quality of the thinking is affected by the equality given to all voices, whether they're sensitive or insensitive. This diversity allows organizations to take the best decisions possible, which will improve the impact that you have on whatever you're trying to do in the world.

Hannah: Do you know of any methods by which to achieve that?

Christine: Yes, for example, say you have a team meeting, and you say to them all, 'OK, this is your chance to contribute.' Not everyone's brain will think of their contribution straight away. Some people need consideration time. But the way we tend to run things is, your chance is now, and if you don't contribute now, then your time is up. And that suits some types of people but passes others by. One of my methods I would suggest is to offer a diversity of ways to contribute and feedback – for example, verbally in the team meeting, or by email before or after the meeting.

Another simple thing is to say, 'OK, what do you think and feel about this?' instead of 'What do you think?' That will hit every preference that is within the listeners. And then really listen to what they have to say, don't interrupt them, don't barge into their speaking or thought processes. Take the time to think about and understand what other people want to say and to offer.

Christine Garner has an incredibly comprehensive on-the-ground and aerial view of the dynamics and realities of work. I liked her description of HSPs as those with extra awareness of what is going on around them: it is clear, simple and gives sensitivity a context for the world of work. I enjoyed her frank dealing with the fact that organizations are, in the main, run in a way that does not support sensitive input, that sensitivity is an underestimated, underused skill. She is right, there is a tremendous amount of hard talk within organizations. And what is very interesting, and Christine Garner got to the heart of it here, is who we invite into the room when we reach moments of 'I don't know what to do next'. We take note from what we consider leadership qualities to be; I think that is who we look to. To go right to the end of an extreme, the type of leadership we vote for, the type we think we need can be summed up in this Donald Trump quote, given during the pre-Capitol insurrection rally speech: 'You will never take back the country with weakness. You have to show strength and you have to stay strong.'

I understand the instinct to follow and seek advice from the super-certain. That confidence. And so I think Christine Garner is right, we leave out of consultations those who are more aware of emotions and impacts on others, those who perhaps take longer to deliberate, who use more uncertain language. The irony implicit in that being that, as explored earlier in this book, the real function of HSPs is as considered decision-makers, long-term planners. And though some HSPs may be in the consultation room where decisions are made, there are not nearly enough.

Speaking to Christine Garner, I am reminded once more of the huge value of skills and intelligence diversity in the workplace. As she says, it makes better products, helps organizations meet the needs of their clients more thoroughly. Any of us who have ever been part of the process of a performance-development review will know it can be daunting to be asked to put language to what you feel your value is, and to hear what your boss thinks your value is. I think it can be incredibly tricky to offer up that you feel part of your value is your sensitivity; and, as Dr Elaine Aron says earlier in this book, it's important to prove your value first. I think the most important thing in what Christine Garner said is, 'I think it's the sensitivity of the sensitive people that will give you the key to selling more and selling better and developing better products and services for a wider proportion of the population; it is not recognized or measured enough, and I think that needs looking at.'

There are millions of HSPs within the workforce around the world, using their skills, often acting as social glue, super-aware of what is going on around them, helping organizations get better at what they do. And pretty much every other skill is given language and a pay point on a performance-development review, but sensitivity is not, even though in many cases it is essential for the role. Meaning that organizations potentially obtain significant added benefit from HSPs without financially rewarding that skill. And that is a problem not only on an individual level, but also for our cultural understanding as to where value sits – because if we have learned nothing else, it is that we value what we put wages next to.

I wanted to find someone to talk to about future jobs economies. For the BBC documentary, we interviewed a professor called David Deming, and I decided it was important to speak to him once again.

———————

David: My name is David Deming. I'm an economist and Professor of Public Policy at the Harvard Kennedy School and Professor of Education and Economics at the Harvard Graduate School of Education. I study the economics of education, labour markets and skills.

Hannah: What are your views about the skill of sensitivity in the labour market, education and skills sector?

David: I think the quality of being able to understand, read and react to other emotions is an important skill. And it's one that's becoming more and more important over time. Some recent research that I've done shows that jobs that require higher levels of social interaction and teamwork have grown as a share of all jobs in the US economy. And they're paying relatively higher wages over the past several decades.

Hannah: What sort of skills do you feel that education systems need to be teaching?

David: I think that the question of whether our schooling system is appropriately preparing young people for society in response to the changing nature of the workplace is an interesting one. To answer that I am going to use my own life as an example.

My children are now aged nine and seven. I still remember when they transitioned from early care into a more formalized school setting. So, first grade – that transition from early care to first grade is dramatic. School really changes and becomes much more individualistic. At preschool, children move around the classroom, in groups often working together on various projects and being guided by the teacher in a way that helps children learn how to play well with each other, and how to share resources and how to negotiate. And then over time, the ideal fifth-grade classroom, for example, starts to look more and more like students sitting at a desk, doing their own work, preparing their own minds for the work they're going to do in the future in a very individual way. That's not the way all schools are, but the majority. And that does not very well prepare young people to think about how to work with others, and knowing how to work with others is a valuable skill.

If you think about how we're judged in school – grades, tests – it's all designed to help evaluate someone's individual performance and contribution. And that's important, because we need to know whether people are doing the work and understanding the work. But then when you look at how people join the workplace, start their first jobs and then progress through their career, there are very few opportunities to evaluate someone's contribution in isolation. What happens is you sort of must learn the essential skill of working on a team, understanding when you're a leader, when you're a follower, when you play different roles. And yes, sure, that is hard for the school system to grade, but it does not mean it is not essential. It does not all need to be about the individual's achievement. The common terming of sensitivity in the workforce skillset is 'social skills'. Terming it as that helps organization leaders understand that this quality, which you describe as sensitivity, has huge value in the workplace economic value, dollars and cents value, right? Of course, it also has moral value. I think we all intuitively know that, but it's important to find a language for it in the language of work and to understand that it makes workers and workplaces more productive.

Hannah: Yes, I can see that. And so, do you feel that there's an ongoing struggle within the business world to hold those things to be of quantifiable value?

David: Well, I do know that we have a bias toward things that we know how to measure and know how to quantify. And certainly, in my home discipline of economics, it's true that we've been very focused for years on what economists would call cognitive skills, or IQ or ability. And these are very loosely captured by a test, like an IQ test or the LSAT or some other tests of problem-solving ability. And because the testing industry has been devoted for many years to developing, refining and perfecting a measure of that, we can use it, and we can understand what the economic returns to that skill are. And we sort of talk about it as if it's the only thing that matters, not because it is the only thing that matters, but because it's the thing we really know how to measure and capture.

We need to start valuing social skills or sensitivity in the same way that we afford privilege to cognitive skills. And I think when we do, we'll discover that being a good team player is just as important to life success.

Businesses are designed with a single purpose, and that is to maximize profits and the value of the business. And, you know, life is so much more than that, and businesses contain humans. We have a range of people in our businesses with strengths and gifts that are not particularly valued or prioritized in the business world. The challenge for us as a society is to make sure that business isn't the only thing that matters.

Hannah: Do you feel there's any advantage in businesses capitalizing on sensitivity?

David: Yes, I do. And I think that's going to be something we're seeing more and more of. There are some job tasks for which a machine can replace a person, and even do much better – in fact there are quite a lot. And they can do it cheaper too. So, an example would be categorizing and processing information, right? If you've got a bunch of data and you want to understand it and the relationships between those data points, or if you want to breed information and summarize it in some way, machines are good at doing that. But then there are lots of job tasks like, let's say I want to understand how best to develop a product. Let's go straight to the business world, I want to develop a product and make it the kind of product that people want to buy. Well, it turns out that being socially sensitive, and understanding what people like and what they don't like, is an important quality, and for things like product design, because you must anticipate what people are going to want. It's an essential human skill. It's hard to see a machine ever replacing that, because the point is to think like another person. And as we get better and better at automating away things that are less human that can be done by machines, work is going to become increasingly the kinds of things that humans are good at and natural at, and it becomes more and more focused on dealing with other humans. That's why the care sector, personal care, personal services have grown so much in every developed country. And I think that will continue to happen apace.

Hannah: It sounds like you feel that we're on the cusp of employment revolution. I was just wondering what kinds of changes you feel employers might need to make.

David: That's a great question. From my perspective, one of the most important, I guess I would call it failures in the market economy right now with care jobs and personal service jobs, is that we really don't understand that much about the underlying skill. And because we don't really understand it, we don't have any way of elevating people who are good at it.

So think about this. Imagine you have elderly parents and let's say that they live the other side of the country, they require care and you can't be there. You are going to want and need someone else to help take care of them as they age. And so, you're thinking about who to hire, whether you're going to hire somebody to live in the home with them or send them to a facility or something else. In making that decision, you're not operating with very much information about who's going to be a good caretaker for your parents or a relative; you don't have much information about what care really means to that caretaker. But you sure would be willing to pay something for that information. If you told me, I'm going to present to you a person who's going to be an excellent caretaker, have real empathy and relationship and integrity in caring for your ageing parents – I bet you would be willing to pay a lot more money for somebody who's good at that than somebody who's mediocre.

And yet, if you look at salaries for home health-workers, they're extraordinarily low. It doesn't seem like people who are good at the job of nursing-home attendant or personal-care worker have a clear career ladder, a way to climb a pay scale in exchange for their valued skillset. There's no way of understanding who's good at that.

And I think that's the crux of the problem, because it's a super-important skill, but we do not understand how to value it yet. In other lines of work, we have ways of understanding what makes someone good at a job. And I think in care work, we're not there yet. So, I think that's a big problem that we need to address.

Part of that low value of the skill of sensitivity is to do with sexism. Women are culturally trained to be good at empathy and care. And empathy and care have traditionally been the domain of women and stay-at-home workers. And because of that, those skills have not been professionalized and understood.

Hannah: So if this were to change, what would need to be done?

David: Well, it really comes down to measurement. How can we quantify care? Develop the language for that? Understand the human value and impact of that? We need a way to measure the skill of care and empathy and sensitivity. Once we can measure it, we can scale it, then we can pay-reward it.

And that is tricky. I can hear the criticisms already in my head, which is oh, you know, it's a soulless economist who wants to quantify the effect that other people have on the care of something that is a human thing. And I'm not saying that we'll ever be able to perfectly measure it, or that by measuring it we have a complete description of all the ways in which good care matters. But I just think making it real means that the business community and the academic community pay attention to it. And I do think, on balance, quantifying something elevates its importance in society. And I'm coming from the perspective of somebody who thinks this work is important and thinks that a world where care work is a bigger part of the economy is a world where we have an incentive to develop social sensitivity and care for each other. That's a better world than what we have right now.

The future of work and its implications for the political system and the future of society is an incredibly important area. One of my I guess not-so-secret-anymore motivations for working on this project was that a world where we value social skills, social intelligence, is a better world, not just for workers, but for us all.

———————

Yes, that is it exactly, Professor Deming: sensitivity as a valued skill offers a potentially better world for us all. There you go, HSPs, our innate trait can potentially make the world a better place. If you didn't feel so great about your trait, please accept that offering. Sensitivity is on the rise; jobs that require teamwork and social interaction are increasingly common, and therefore the ability to understand, read and react to others' emotions will become increasingly vital. I suppose in a similar vital role to that of our evolutionary past.

So how do we do that? What is clear from talking to Professor Deming is that the 'how' is measurement. We value what we can measure. So even though sensitivity is quite a complex, unquantifiable thing, we do need to start quantifying it. For its own good. What do we do when we don't know how to measure something? We innovate. That is what he is doing, and as he says, it's bound to be imperfect the first time round. But in development is a strong start. Let's redistribute some of the privilege afforded to measured skills – give sensitivity a spot of time in the sun. Not at the cost of the other skills we measure and value, but alongside them.

Writing this chapter, I realize I have been smiling. I think it is relief and gratefulness that there are these individuals out there, noticing, understanding, changing things. I think back to my daughter at playgroup, doing laps around the room observing the activity at length before participating. I think back to past me worrying, mortified that she was not doing what the other kids were. If I could have a chat with my past so-very-worried self, I would say, Hannah, don't worry, the world she will live in is different to the one you have lived in, in some terrifying ways and in some ways that are so long overdue. There is a place for her and all the others.

10. Why is it in us?

So why are we sensitive? Why do we as a species have this trait? I want to know if sensitivity is in us because it was useful in the past. Unfortunately, I cannot interview the past. But what I can do is interview anthropological archaeologists – those who seek to explore the human past, including the origin and evolution of culture, inequality, agriculture and urban life, and link this past life to the life we live today. Basically, anthropological archaeologists examine the story of human beings, sometimes by looking at cultures in the present to understand the past. I decided to begin with talking to Dr David Chicoine, Associate Professor at Louisiana State University. We briefly dated a long time ago and I have followed his work with interest since.

David: My name is Dr David Chicoine. I am an anthropological archaeologist who studies ancient Andean societies. My field research focuses on the north coast of Peru, and I currently direct excavations at Cerro San Isidro in the Nepeña Valley.

Hannah: David, why is sensitivity part of us as a species?

David: To answer that I think we must think about the component parts of sensitivity, like empathy, cooperation. I think we must ask the question, how did that develop in our ancestors? When did modern cognition happen? Because we know, through looking at our closest ancestors, that sensitivity, empathy, cooperation are part of modern cognition. So basically, around 1.7 million years ago to around a million years ago, when our ancestors transitioned from archaic hominins such as Australopithecines and *Homo habilis* to *Homo ergaster* and *erectus*, from having a brain size that was much closer to chimpanzees to a brain size of 1000 cubic centimetres, much closer to our species – that is when we start to see innovations like fire, complex tools, systematic big-game hunting. The origin of aesthetics and art. Ellen Dissanayake says in her book *What is Art for?*:

> ...from very early (as long ago as 200,000 years), humans have been naturally attracted to the extraordinary as a dimension of experience and that at some point they seem also to have been moved to make the ordinary extraordinary – that is, to shape or elaborate everyday, mundane reality and thereby transform it into something special, different from the everyday.

So basically, and as pointed out by Denis Dutton in his book *The Art Instinct*, the origin of our cognition coincides with when we became able to tell stories that didn't exist and make people believe that they exist. And this had an evolutionary advantage, because our minds could adapt and be better prepared to face the unknown. And empathy, socially or interpersonally, could help you be prepared to deal with all kinds of situations in a reactive way. As well as art, empathy and cooperation are traits that use the skill of sensitivity. You should read *Mothers and Others: The Evolutionary Origins of Mutual Understanding* by Sarah Blaffer Hrdy.

And how did we get to a place where we had decreased value in sensitivity? It is, of course, difficult to identify a single moment in the past when things changed...There was a whole shift in thinking post the Enlightenment. Descartes had a lot of responsibility for putting the idea out there that there's a real empirical world that we should be observing with actual, physical, objective tools. And then developments such as there are natural laws out there that exist that we can observe, like gravity, physics.

I was recently writing a paper for a conference about Karl Polanyi, the Hungarian political economist, historian and journalist. He wrote a book about the great transformation of the origin of market economy and industrialization and how that basically led to all kinds of problems in the 20th century, like fascism. What he points out is the fact that market economies, when they were created in the early 19th century, were backed up by a series of thinkers who claimed that this was the natural law. That came at the cost of other values and other ways of thinking. The idea emerged of free-market economy, of let the market decide. That's when Darwin, Tylor, Spencer and others came up with the concept of evolution by natural selection and coined the phrase 'survival of the fittest', the idea that the market would basically weed out the weak.

You probably read the work of Michel Foucault, especially his contribution to body politics. Because we talk about education and how education disciplines bodies to be less sensitive. In his book on discipline and punishment, he traces the history of three institutions: the prison, the school and hospitals. He shows that they are basically the same model, places where we are training bodies to become useful bodies in the capitalist economy. In terms of the devaluing of sensitivity, if we look at who gets paid well in our current society, it's not hard to understand that if you are a humanist, a writer, a musician, you are not going to be paid as much or as valued as, for example, a scientist or a banker, where it is advantageous to have more empirical evidence, less emotion required as part of the job role.

Marilyn Strathern wrote a book called *The Gender of the Gift*. And that book really proposed the idea that in many societies, the way that people see themselves, it's not as individuals but as a group where you connect with others, whether they are your ancestors, your family members, kin or children, because you share substances, you eat the same thing, you take part in the same activities, and that is a power – one group, one entity. And things like witchcraft, often these practices have a lot to do with this. Because you can impact one body by dealing with another body. And so, sensitivity within that context is useful in that it enables you to connect, to identify and to move with the needs of the group. And that is very different from how most of us live now.

So why is this in us? Because sensitivity was a good skill and strategy to use. It's quite simple really. Sensitivity, I am increasingly coming to understand, works as an umbrella term for actions such as cooperation and empathy. They have the shared root of sensitivity, it takes the skill of sensitivity to act with empathy, it takes the skill of sensitivity to cooperate successfully.

Dr David Chicoine said a few things in his interview that were new thoughts to me. And no, David, I had not read Foucault or Descartes, but after your suggestions I did. And yes, I can see a really clear line in the sand, whereby a certain set of skills were presented as useful and others, such as sensitivity, were deprioritized. I am fascinated by David's mention of the role of the arts and storytelling, that they emerged at the same time as modern cognition, at the same time as evidenced cooperation, increased empathy and so on. What does that tell us about the importance of the arts to culture and society? I wonder how many artists are highly sensitive?

I am curious about this idea that the arts – storytelling – prepare us to face the unknown by using our imagination muscles to help us imagine other realities. I can indeed see how useful this is in facing the unknown: flexible minds open to possibility, rehearsed alternative scenarios. It makes me wonder how unhelpful a static mindset is to us as a species, to keep with the idea that 'this is how things are and this is how they will stay'. It makes me think of the skills that Lord Knight (back in chapter 4) said were useful for the future – agency, change resilience, flexibility. I think of a Sunday afternoon I spent watching the cartoon *The Croods*, not long after I had given birth to my daughter. I watched it with my stepdaughter, who was then fourteen, and my partner. It is about a family of cave people living in an environment which is ending, under significant threat, and they have gone into hiding. The father's mantra is 'new is always bad' – to keep your head down and hide, keep things the same, is the best survival strategy. But it is not working, and it looks as if the family will perish. Suddenly a stranger comes into their environment and shows them that by reinventing, using imagination and change-resilience, they can dodge disaster, move on and find a new existence.

After watching the cartoon, our fourteen-year-old turned to us and said, 'So basically, we survived as a species because we learned how to adapt?' We said 'Yes.'

And she said, 'And to realize there is a problem you need to be sensitive, to be able to notice there is a problem?'

'Yes.'

'So to adapt you need to be sensitive?'

'Yes'.

'Well, shouldn't they teach us that instead of it all being about passing tests all the time?'

We had no real answer for her.

***

The capacity to imagine different realities, the curiosity to create new innovations, the ability to cooperate, to care for one another – those are skills that should not be underestimated or easily dismissed. They are powerful tools, exceptional skills, and we all have the capacity to use them, to best develop them. I have never considered human consciousness and development as being like a muscle that hones traits and benefits from stretching through stories, through imagination. But it makes perfect sense, and roots for me the value of the arts as something that is a vital part of society's health and resilience.

What skills help us to face the unknown – to step into it and to start innovating? I wonder about the role of story in teaching this. What power do the stories that we tell hold? What stories do we ingest? We live among a lot of hero stories, singular winners who triumph. But among those stories there are a scant few alternatives. We have this story in my mum's side of the family.

It was told by my grandad, Professor John Northam – we called him Da. He told the story to my mum and her three brothers, then he told it to me, my siblings and cousins, and now we tell it to our children. And I have been wondering about its function. Sure, perhaps it is just a story, a nice story for soothing and entertaining. But I think it might mean something more. It goes like this:

> There was this Bear called Bear. And every morning he got out of bed, put both feet on the floor, stretched, put on his bow tie, skipped down the stairs singing, 'Oh the world owes me a living, toodle oodle oo.' And makes himself a boiled egg and soldiers for breakfast, and then heads out the door to walk the town. And as he goes he lists the names of plants and trees he sees around him, so water mint, silver birch, twisted willow, until he reaches the right field, and that is the one with the giant tree in it, and in that field is a maze of rabbit warrens and the bear wriggles his way through the tunnels, past worms and bricks until he comes to a kingdom, and that is the kingdom of the greenie brownie king and the diamond queen.

Then Da would stop, look at us full of mirth and ask, 'And what happens next?' He would pause and wait and then slowly repeat, 'What happens next?' It was our job to come up with what happens next. It didn't matter what we offered, the point was we took over the telling and did it together. The point was it increased our confidence in inventing, in taking the new space that was offered to us.

The answers we gave were sometimes silly – things like there's a dancing bee. Sometimes they were more profound – like the king and the queen have an argument and must figure out how to co-rule. I suppose we put into the holes of that story whatever our lived experience was at the time, and then it was stretched, our imaginations were stretched. We were told that story so many times that it is in us all. We all know it. I sometimes dream about it – this long gap, where Da is looking at me kindly and saying, 'What happens next, what happens next?' And I am not filled with panic at the thought of needing to come up with what happens next. I feel like he trained us all up with the skill of inventive imagination.

When he told us that story, he always sat in a green velvet armchair, and while he was thinking he would run his fingers across the ends of the arms of the chair. Back and forth, back and forth, while he waited for our answers. There were threadbare worn patches where his fingers had run over and over. He was part of a working-class generation given access to an upper-class education due to so many young men having died in the First World War. Though his mother grew up in the workhouse, he was given scholarships, went to Cambridge and devoted the rest of his career to the university and the critical study of Ibsen the playwright. I think, and I wish I had asked, that he believed for his children and grandchildren in the power of what you work at, the power of developing muscles of imagination. I think he believed in the power of handing children information and giving them agency, I think he believed in the power of story to transform the present, in giving agency and power to face change.

Stories aside, I am struck and surprised by Dr David Chicoine's explanation that sensitivity played a large role in human brain expansion, the splitting away in development from our closest ancestors coinciding with the moment in development where skills such as innovation and cooperation started to become a more established part of us. The idea that as our brains and societies expanded, we needed greater awareness of interpersonal communication so that we didn't continuously act with aggression towards one another. How to live alongside one another, how to bear proximity – I mean, that is still an ongoing concern among communities. The skills needed to live together in a community are complex, and it makes sense that that is partly what sensitivity is for.

David suggested that I read *Mothers and Others* by Professor Sarah Blaffer Hrdy and so I did. Her work combines comparative primatology, developmental and evolutionary psychology, and ethnographic data. *Mothers and Others* looks at the evolution of the human species and the length of human childhood and concludes that raising a human child is expensive in terms of time and resource. It explores the fact that to raise a child successfully relies on distributing this cost among community, so that the young are cared for, not only by their mothers, but by an extended community consisting of friends, siblings, grandparents, and so on. This is termed alloparenting. Professor Hrdy argues that an important skill in such a setup is the ability to differentiate between who will care for us and who will not, and that this requires developing the skills to detect quite complex social and emotional cues. She makes the case that a consequence of this was the development of our capacity for understanding others' emotions and motives. She argues that this is significantly different to what happened with our closest ancestors.

Her work shows how vital it would therefore have been to one's wellbeing and chances of survival to develop skills such as extreme empathy, detailed reading of facial cues and body language. She suggests that the reason humans developed the large white bits of our eyes is their extended capacity for expressiveness. She basically makes the case that our heightened emotional sensitivity was vital to our survival in a setup where parenting was not just done by mothers.

Parenting nowadays is expensive; it is mainly solo, it is practically almost impossible to work full time. But millions of us do it. Have we evolved from a society of shared parenting cost into a culture of solo parenting cost? How fascinating, how contradictory, how ironic. If we evolved this trait of sensitivity, or rather honed and developed it as the result of cooperative breeding culture, that means we are wired for empathy, understanding and reading of others as part of a survival strategy. The implications of that, evolutionarily, politically, are gigantic.

Increasingly I am growing uneasy, angry even, that we are currently presented with a narrative that says that the dominant traits essential for our survival are aggression, dominance and competition. When the fact that we are here now as a species can also be understood as the result of development of the skills of and capacity for sensitivity. Where is that story? Why do we not have that narrative too? Too female? What a load of shit. A narrative that says, look, the skill of sensitivity has been a useful part of our survival is not just important for understanding our history, it's important for those of us living now, those of us who are living without that support system.

I remember standing at the window of our tenement flat in Edinburgh, on a snowy day, my one-year-old daughter asleep on my shoulder. The outside had become a white room. I stood and looked at how beautiful everything had become, how transformed. I watched the snowflakes falling for a long time. And I felt this root pull, this aching for community, for my siblings – it was as if my heart was out on a lead trying to reach for them. I needed to keep working, for my spirit and for the economy of our household. Never has it been clearer to me the immeasurable value of those who can hold out a hand to help, even if only a little. That is why we moved back to be near to them. I wonder how many mothers – fathers, too, but mainly mothers – are on their own, trying to keep their heads above water, and I feel the urge to shout, this feels hard because it's not meant to be this way, it's not always been this way. It's not just you who finds this almost impossible, it's the system, it's the story, and the story is nonsense. And I wonder once again, who stands to benefit from keeping in place the story that we need to live and achieve, to raise our children in competitive silos?

Sarah Blaffer Hrdy's book suggests a different order of values – one where it is advantageous to us as a species to understand one another emotionally, through the whites of our eyes, detailed facial expression, intuition. This makes our understanding of sensitivity something central to our development, vital even. Looking at the trait and skill of sensitivity from this angle, I have begun to feel a little less sorry for it. It has older, deeper roots. It is integral to us all. More entwined with us than we have language and story for. It feels, suddenly, quite profound.

I am taken by this notion of collectivity. Dame Marilyn Strathern's idea that in many societies we have a different concept of ourselves as a group – sharing substances, food, activities – a power, one entity. The thought that sensitivity allows you to connect, to identify, to move with the needs of the group, is very different to how we live now. It's an entirely different concept of individuality and community, togetherness and singularity.

We currently live in the story of bigger, better, more – we are told that this is natural law. But that is not entirely true. Dr David

Chicoine took the time to explain some reasons why sensitivity value decreased: industrialism (again), capitalism, market economy. I was struck by him mentioning that when the market economy was created, it was backed up by thinkers who claimed it as the natural law. Just in case you don't know – market economy is a system we currently live in, where someone wants something and another person provides it – supply and demand. Market economy promotes cut-throat competition as its main value. It promotes survival of the fittest. It drives down the cost of goods. It allows economic inequality, unemployment, monopolistic suppliers who, with the advantage of scale, drive down the cost of goods at the expense of smaller suppliers. Fascinating that the birth of that idea was accompanied by a story that said, 'This is the way it's always been.' The power of story to radically shape what we believe. It is a form of gaslighting, in fact, and is one of the moments when our understanding of values such as sensitivity started to go fundamentally awry. Our understanding of what was important became that of what can we measure, what can we sell, who will survive?

David Chicoine also touched on the value with which we educate and how that connects to the economy. The idea that we have educational and correctional facilities that train bodies to become less sensitive in the name of becoming useful to the capitalist economy. And he is right: look at who gets paid well, look at what professions are held as the epitome of success – scientists, bankers, those whose jobs rely on empirical evidence. Jobs such as carers, artists, humanists rely on less quantifiable, less well understood qualities such as sensitivity. I am struck by how difficult we as a species seem to find it to deal with the unknown, the intangible – our tendency towards knowns and quantifiables – and I wonder what the emotional need is at the root of that impulse. Is it fear? What do we tell ourselves is essential when we are hit with a time of hardship? Well, to use the pandemic as an example – the economy was put first. The sectors left to hang under-resourced included the care sector and teaching, and the jobs cut were from the arts. I leave this interview with David Chicoine thinking about how we have relied on sensitivity as a key part of our development, but split ourselves apart from it recently, in order for a different kind of story to thrive. Can multiple stories exist at the same time? Or does one need to come at the cost of the other? Surely, we have the capacity to hold both to be simultaneously true.

I decided that next I wanted to interview someone who works researching cultures in other parts of the world, outside the Western system. So, I set out on the hunt and found the perfect candidate literally on my geographical doorstep.

Nikhil: My name is Dr Nikhil Chaudhary, I am a lecturer in human evolutionary and behavioural ecology at Cambridge University in the Department of Archaeology. I completed my PhD and postdoctoral research as a member of the Hunter-Gatherer Resilience Project, which examined the cultural and behavioural adaptations of hunter-gatherer societies in Africa and Asia.

I work principally with the Mbendjele BaYaka hunter-gatherers, a Pygmy population residing in the rainforests of Northern Congo. My research thus far has explored the role of cooperative networks and non-kin relationships in human evolution; human life-history evolution; and the relationship between social structure and cultural transmission. I have a special interest in evolutionary psychology.

Hannah: Thank you, Nikhil. So what can you tell me about how other cultures value sensitivity?

Nikhil: To understand if there are other cultures that value sensitivity differently, you have to first ask what is sensitivity and why does sensitivity exist as a trait at all? How did this trait evolve? Sensitivity, from a biological perspective, is basically the extent to which you detect and respond to stimuli in the environment. And broadly speaking, the two relevant types of stimuli for survival and reproduction are physical stimuli and social stimuli. We can talk about both, but I imagine what you mean by sensitivity refers principally to the latter – our emotional responses to social stimuli. Throughout most of our history we have lived as hunter-gatherers and, on the most basic level, being able to respond to stimuli appropriately is incredibly valuable to our survival, if we think of sensitivity as responsiveness.

There is this idea of the smoke-detector principle. It's basically the idea that you can make false-positive or negative errors when you're making a judgement, when you're trying to detect something in the environment and respond to it. For example, if you hear a noise behind you, maybe that noise is just some leaves rustling, or maybe it's a predator. And the cost of thinking it's leaves rustling when it's a predator is extremely high – this would be a false-negative error. Now, the cost of being oversensitive and making a false-positive error, that is, thinking it's a predator and acting accordingly, when in fact it is just leaves rustling, is minimal, so it's cost-effective. It's sort of a good strategy, because usually not responding to things is much more costly than false alarms. And the reason it's called the smoke-detector principle is like, just think about with a fire alarm: you'd much rather design a fire alarm to be a bit paranoid – hypersensitive, with the occasional false alarm – than have one which is a bit under-sensitive, and risk not being warned when there is an actual fire.

Which moves us into the idea of how sensitivity got its negativity. Well, because sometimes it probably causes some distress to the person, the experience is not necessarily a pleasant one, like reacting to conditions that are not suitable for us. And the law of psychology, and even psychiatry, to some degree has been based in this paradigm, that things that feel good are good, and things that feel bad are bad, right?

But there's this concept of diagonal psychology, which I think makes sense from an evolutionary perspective, which is that, ultimately, we have negative emotions and positive emotions and that there's a reason for that. Evolution didn't shape our psychology and our emotions to feel nice. It shaped them for survival and reproduction. And in certain contexts, feeling negative feelings is useful. If we weren't sensitive or if we didn't feel nervousness or anxiety, we'd be in a lot of trouble. You would not be having appropriate reactions to harmful situations around you.

In a similar way for those with illnesses like leprosy that prevent them from feeling physical pain in their extremities, – keeping their hand in a flame is damaging – pain is useful to us, it tells us often what not to do. It's dangerous to not have that inbuilt appropriate reaction. Everything we see in humans is something that's evolved. To be clear – when you say sensitivity, I understand that and study it in its component parts of behaviour – empathy, cooperation, social sensitivity, as well as physical sensory sensitivity.

Sensitivity, in this social and behavioural sense, may well

be the main reason for the size of our big brains as a species. There are a couple of things evolutionary biologists would say have allowed humans to colonize the globe. There are very few single species, probably none, which are as successful as ours, and it's largely due to the fact that we are hyper-cooperative. You certainly see cooperation in other animals, but often it's more restricted and tends to happen among close genetic relatives. I'd say the leading hypothesis as to why we have a big brain is for sensitivity, and social sensitivity and empathy. Now, it's not phrased using those words in my profession, it's called the social-brain hypothesis. And it's basically that if you look across primates, like humans, other apes and monkeys, you can see that brain size is basically predicted by the social-group size and the complexity of social dynamics, which suggests that the function of brain evolution and expansion was principally driven by social factors. The reason we have these big brains is that it helps us navigate complex social interactions. You may have heard of theory of mind? So, theory of mind is basically the ability to understand other people's emotions, their perspective and motivations.

For example, you and I are having this discussion. We don't treat each other as inanimate objects, we recognize that the other has a mind. I understand that, right now, what you're seeing is not what I'm seeing. I'm seeing your face, but you are seeing mine, so I can understand your visual perspective and that it's different to mine. And the one thing that humans are super good at is taking other people's emotional and motivational perspective. So, I attune to and am sensitive to how you're feeling and why you might behave in a particular way. We as a species are very good at this, like mind-reading. The more I can take your perspective, the more empathetic I'm going to be; the more empathetic I am, the more appropriate my responses will be. And I think the predominant hypothesis for why humans have big brains is so that we can navigate complex social problems and live in these big social groups.

Part of the reason that humans are so good at collaborating – and in biology, collaboration is slightly different to cooperation; collaboration is that we can work together for a shared goal, a joint goal – is that we use our theory of mind in the context of collaborative activities. So if I'm trying to achieve something, which I can't do on my own, but I could do if we work together, obviously that requires us to coordinate our behaviour. For example, to lift something, to get some food, we need to be able to communicate well, when to lift, or if you're struggling and need a break, be attuned to the other and what is going to be most helpful. So, we use empathy, this sensitivity to other people's perspectives and emotions, as a way for collaboration to thrive. And that type of cooperation and collaboration is unrivalled in the animal kingdom.

So, when you're thinking about empathy and sensitivity, it wouldn't be inappropriate to say that these are among the principal functions of humans' large brains and the human brain expansion. That is one of the major factors to have contributed to our evolutionary success and uniqueness as a species, because we have this capacity to be sensitive to one another's perspective and emotions and goals, enabling us to be so much better able to collaborate and live in cooperative societies.

Hannah: I think what is amazing about what you have just told me is that sensitivity in its component parts (empathy, care, cooperation) is fundamental to our success and evolution as a species.

Nikhil: Yes, it's vital. Of course, there are cases where someone's sensitive reaction to something is problematic. There is, of course, a point in sensitivity, as with everything, where it can become dysfunctional. I'm not saying that the more sensitive you are, the better. I am saying our ability to be sensitive to a degree is responsible for our success as a species and may also explain why we have such big brains.

Hannah: Nikhil, in your research have you learned of other cultures past or present that value sensitivity differently?

Nikhil: Yes. I found in hunter-gatherer societies that people who are better able to form authentic social alliances have more children and are healthier, because cooperation and integrity are so vital. People have argued that it's not real cooperation, but false offerings for personal gain as a strategy, which we would interpret, if at a high level, as sociopathy – the ability to manipulate another while pretending, to get what we want for our personal gain. But there is some interesting evidence that sort of behaviour does not do very well in hunter-gatherer societies. If you're behaving in a selfish way, being a taker and not a giver, particularly if you try and express any form of dominance, you just have no chance. Hunter-gatherers live in egalitarian societies. So, there's no formal hierarchy at all. And if someone tries to behave in a dominant way, or take away someone else's autonomy, they are immediately rebutted by the collective.

Autonomy is important to the culture – you can't even

really tell kids what to do in the way that we do in our culture. If someone committed the crime of dominance and selfishness, there is a series of processes to put that person back in their place – it begins with verbal ridicule and moves on to ritualistic mockery and ostracism. So, say I had been trying to be the big man and wanted to keep all the food to myself or was boasting in some way, when I came into camp, usually women will sit outside their homes and re-enact my behaviour in front of me with everyone laughing. It's a way of saying we notice the way you're behaving and we're not going to have it; if you continue like this, things can get a bit more severe than ridicule.

In our society being dominant, or behaving insensitively, is not punished, we sort of accept it. And it's not really something that has important implications for us at this moment in time, because once you live in the market economy you are not dependent on cooperation. Whereas in hunter-gatherer societies there's so much unpredictability in whether you're going to have a successful hunt one day to the next, whether there will be food; and if you don't have many alliances, you're in real trouble. But if you've got alliances, it means on the days I don't catch food, you will give me some of yours. And the days I get food, I'll give you some of mine. The market economy is the opposite to that; the market economy is based on dominance and competition. No hunter-gatherer families would survive if they tried to implement the values of the market economy. You cannot keep resources to yourself, compete and be dominant, and then the next day say, oh, sorry, I didn't get any food today, do you mind if I have some of yours, so I don't starve?

Hunter-gatherer societies don't build hierarchies, because

everyone's so dependent on each other. Rather than hierarchy, which tends to be triangular, where you've got like the alpha, and then a few betas, and a few people below them – that triangle, it's inverted, where any one individual who tries to be dominant is then dominated by the collective. It's called reverse hierarchy. And these mechanisms are called levelling mechanisms – ridicule, ostracism and potentially execution in certain cases are basically an expression of complete rejection of dominant behaviour, some anthropologists say. And some of the positive ways that those behaviours are entrenched is through societal storytelling: we also found that camps with good storytellers had a higher degree of cooperation, less selfish behaviour, and the storytellers themselves had more children and more people wanting to cooperate with them, meaning they had more prestige. Storytelling is quite an important cultural mechanism of encouraging cooperation within the group. For example, a lot of stories are about caricatured animals and what they teach us – the one that behaved selfishly loses out in the end, the one that didn't prevails, and so forth.

Also, the games children play in hunter-gatherer societies are based on the behaviour they see in their community. It is never competitive, it is cooperative. For example, they will play and work together to turn a low tree into a seesaw or something. In our society children are competitive, organized activity is competitive sport. Sure, you get collaboration between children in our society too, but they are sort of trained and streamlined to compete, to get ready for the market economy, which seems harmless on the surface, it's just children's games, but what it means, what the basics are of the values we teach, is bigger and deeper than just playing.

What is valued or allows one to be successful in our societies is really the antithesis of what would have been a good strategy for more than 95 per cent of our history when we were living as hunter-gatherers.

So much of the values of a society depend on how they are culturally embedded. Where I work there is so much solidarity, not just through group living, but also through rituals of unity. For example, there is a ritual where everyone comes together for group singing and dancing. One thing you see in rituals around the world, in traditional societies, is there tends to be synchronous movement and chanting. You see it often in religious gatherings; for example, in a mosque Muslims will be in synchrony during bowing. But even football fans have ritualistic synchronous chanting. It seems to be a highly conserved cultural practice, which is so interesting, because they've shown on a physiological level how good that is for the central nervous system to calm down, to tell your body this is safe, you are safe. And during these group singing and movement practices people's endorphins have been measured, and it has been shown that they are physiologically bonding with one another. There is something in the process of synchrony that creates a sort of identity fusion; the collective merges with your identity, you are a part of something, therefore the idea of competition and dominance, which is about the individual working against the unit, does not fit or work.

—————————

To unpack that interview a little. Sensitivity is understood in evolutionary biology as responsiveness to environment, same as in neuroscience and psychology. We have lived as hunter-gatherers for most of our history as a species on Earth. What is valued now in the society we have created is the opposite of what would have been considered good strategy for 95 per cent of our history. So what do we mean by good strategy? Something that would keep us as safe as possible, give us the best bet of survival. A lot of our survival and wellbeing in the past was dependent on others, community groups. We do not currently have that understanding, we live in conventional units, in silos. By looking at hunter-gatherer societies that still exist, we can understand that the values of the past were different out of necessity. That those with authentic social alliances have more children and are healthier – considered signs of success. Storytelling roles are held in esteem. Cooperation is so important to the values of that society that if you do not share or cooperate there are consequences, big ones. Autonomy and non-hierarchical structures are considered important, completely the opposite of our education system. Belonging to the group is so much more important, for the individual and the group, that it is enforced – that is an idea I have never encountered before. I cannot help but feel how very opposite this is to our society, as our autonomy and hierarchies grow more rigid with things such as the right to peaceful protest becoming against the law. The market economy does rest on competition and conformity. And I can see how the monopoly of that story of market economy, presented as 'this is how it's always been', has come at the cost of other values. I am struck by the fact that collectively we all now stand on the precipice of the unknown, facing big global problems. And we all need to make it. Don't we?

So how do we do that? Do we keep doing things the way the market economy teaches us, that the way out of this is to compete or ignore it? Or do we have other resources we can draw on, ones we have overlooked or overwritten? What do we do in the face of the unknown? To find an example of this you need only think back to March 2020, to the announcement that we were going into lockdown, and supermarket shelves were stripped bare, with old people pleading for others to please leave something in the shops for them too. We are so afraid that we will not help each other. We have so little trust that we will be cared for. That is what our economy has taught us. We are atomized, we are solo units, with rare examples of community. That is how we live.

So that is why I find the idea of rituals of unity that Dr Nikhil Chaudhary mentioned so fascinating. That all religions and non-religions have synchronous movement built in. It had never occurred to me that this has a positive effect on your nervous system. That it tells your body, you are OK, this is safe. I am really interested in the idea of the process of synchronous movement and chanting that makes people bond, that means people understand themselves as part of a whole. And that neutralizes the idea that dominance and competition are the best strategies. It takes the use of the skill of sensitivity to understand and hold us.

I feel moved by the idea that you can tell the values of a society by looking at the games children play. That our current system teaches competitive play, which seems harmless on the surface but has implications much bigger and deeper than we perhaps understand. It is interesting that in hunter-gatherer societies, play is predominantly cooperative. My daughter takes issue with competitive play – 'I will race you to see who can get dressed before the other' or 'See how many star jumps you can do before you fall over' – it sends her into real panic. Sometimes she even says, 'It makes my heart feel funny', probably because it stresses out her nervous system. Dr Nikhil Chaudhary emphasized this in his interview – the method by which our values are embedded. The methods he described are storytelling and group activity. I have been trying to think by what methods current values are instilled, and I am at a loss. As a storyteller myself, I cannot help but be slightly pleased that there are societies out there where skills like mine have greater value than they do in our own. Storytelling teaches critical thinking skills, questioning, philosophy and empathy – all of which support cooperation.

It is also interesting that Dr Nikhil Chaudhary touched on some of the same areas as Dr David Chicoine. The idea that the size of our brains correlates with the size of the group we are required to live in and the need for complex interpersonal skills. Theory of mind being the ability to understand other thoughts and feelings alongside our own. The more I can take your perspective, the more empathic I will be, the more appropriate my response will be. And we are back again to what Dr Bianca Acevedo the neuroscientist told us in chapter 7 about appropriate response and sensitivity. Sensitivity, in short, allows us to create things greater than ourselves, things like societies, structures, systems and projects.

Dr Nikhil Chaudhary told me that for 95 per cent of our lived history as a species, skills that umbrella out from sensitivity have been the best survival strategy for us all. In terms of how we live together, what the structure is of those societies, and in terms of danger-reading. The smoke-detector principle that he described. The idea that if you hear a noise behind you, turning around to look is a relatively cheap action if it turns out to be a twig falling. Versus you hear a noise behind you, you don't look and it turns out to be a predator. Expensive action, high cost. Sensitivity as a strategy is relatively cheap, guarding us against unnecessary risk, giving us the best chance of survival. It is in all our interests to look behind us to see what that noise is. But currently those who are most likely to turn around are told that they are weak for wanting to do so, their propensity for being most likely to notice danger is dismissed. No wonder HSPs struggle with their mental health. There is an inbuilt system that says, jump if you notice danger; HSPs jump and are told they are weak for jumping. In our society we reward non-reactiveness, stoicism and an emotional stiff upper lip; it would be much easier to be an HSP if we understood collectively that there is a reason we are jumping, that it is part of how we are made.

As Dr Nikhil Chaudhary said, we need diversity, and I agree. I am not advocating for our entire society to be run by the values or personalities of HSPs. We need diversity, I cannot stress that enough; however, we currently have the narrative that there is one best way to be a strong and successful person, and one set of values that is innate to us. That is what needs to fundamentally change.

So, to add to the story a little bit more – sensitivity was more useful to us in the past. It had more roles attributed to it in a more widespread, intrinsic way. Sensitivity was a sound navigational, situational, survival skill. It is an old skill, a big capacity in us all. It is more integral to our identity than we understand it to be.

I want to return to the interview I conducted with Dr Elaine Aron (see chapter 3), in which she touches on the evolutionary value of the sensitive.

———————————

Hannah: What do you think the evolutionary advantage is of being sensitive?

Elaine: Sensitive individuals notice what the majority do not. If everyone was equally sensitive, equally aware of opportunities, there'd be no value in anyone being sensitive. Because there is a cost to being highly sensitive – to noticing what others miss. It takes time and brain power. For example, you are in a traffic jam, and you think you know a shortcut. You enjoy looking at maps or exploring your neighbourhood, noticing how things are laid out. A highly sensitive person might be like that. Most drivers would not bother. But if every driver knows the shortcut, then it's not an advantage anymore.

Or imagine two animals, one that notices differences in the nutrition of patches of grass, one that does not. If the differences are not very great, there is no advantage. Noticing is irrelevant. A waste of the sensitive animal's time. And if all the animals noticed that some patches were better than others, the best ones would be eaten up quickly and there would be no advantage to being sensitive to those differences. But if some notice and others don't, and sometimes the differences are big, the ones noticing are getting an advantage.

Hannah: So, it's a survival strategy?

Elaine: It is a survival strategy. It is exactly a survival strategy. But it's an advantage for myself. It's not an advantage for a group. It's one that works for a certain percentage.

Hannah: What do you think the advantage is to the rest of the population? Having HSPs among them?

Elaine: I really think that humans must get over this instinctive ranking of one group as better than the other. I hope it is something that highly sensitive people can lead in. It must help that marginalized groups are stepping forward and saying, 'Well, look at how great we really are.' Individuals in minority groups need to be given a chance. And that's where avoiding stereotypes comes in. Each person is different with different talents, whatever group they belong to. I think that businesses are learning that, that they need to look at each of their employees as unique assets. HSPs also must learn to explain their skills better. That all depends on the situation, of course. Sometimes it will work to say, 'Yes, I am sensitive, in the sense that I think deeply about things. That means I'm creative and I see the big picture. I'm sure you have also noticed that I have good social skills.' But it works best to bring up these things after you've proven they are true, proven your worth at a certain level. I have often found that sensitive people don't realize how valued they are by their organization, that they can ask for things that they need.

That said, it is easy to imagine how respecting and promoting HSPs in an organization could improve its functioning. I remember someone saying about a US President who makes quick decisions, even if they are wrong, that he is more respected than one who thinks it over before deciding and then is right. Since an HSP likes to think things over, that would take some getting used to, but if HSPs were clear about the value of slowing down, it might work. I met someone who was a consultant in Washington, DC, and he just was appalled by how little people thought things through before they acted. I have written about this Indo-European type of government in which you have the warrior kings and the priestly advisors. A modern example would be in the US, the Executive Branch and Supreme Court. The advisors are there to slow down the people who think they need to make quick decisions. It's the big picture that is often missing. In every field of human endeavour, quick decision-making, which sometimes does have value, needs to be balanced with slow deliberation, even if it is after the fact, when what happened is reconsidered and new approaches will be applied next time. So those with high sensitivity and those without the trait should work together, respecting each other.

HSPs need to be aware of what value they add to any organization and then find a way to exert more influence in that organization. As for how HSPs should be treated in an organization to get the best from them (their deepest and most creative ideas), you must give them what they need. But the fact is, usually what they need would be best for everybody, such as a quiet place to work with some natural light, clean air, good food nearby. Everybody needs it, but HSPs are the ones who notice when it is lacking.

Here's a good example: HSPs do better if most of the feedback they receive is positive. That is true for most people, highly sensitive or not. But HSPs pay special attention to positive feedback. They learn from it and feel calmer and happier when they hear it, and thus can be more productive. They pay attention to negative feedback too (they are not being 'too sensitive', because paying close attention to all feedback is normal for them, part of their special survival strategy). But they may overreact to the negative – for example, redoing something when it did not need it or holding back suggestions in the future. They may also leave the organization, having found it too anxiety-provoking or just that it did not appreciate them. 'It was not a good fit', when in fact it could have been if a little bit more effort had been made to understand their needs and meet them.

Dr Elaine Aron is right; we really do need to get over this idea that one group is better than another. Her evolutionary explanation of HSPs is the first I have encountered that considers the benefit for the individual of being highly sensitive – it is a personal survival strategy. We notice things others might not. That should be the slogan of HSPs. I can see it embroidered on badges, flags, tattoos. It is a survival strategy, one that not only benefits the group in terms of values, but also benefits the individuals. And if we were all to use the strategy of those with the trait of HSPs, it would cease to be successful. Every species on Earth has a unique survival strategy. Some living in air, some in water, some on land. Some fast, some slow. Some tough, some sensitive. That is a much better story for sensitivity, that it is part of a matrix of methods for survival. If we all did it the same, it would be at a cost.

We have long believed in the dominant narrative of survival of the fittest, the strongest, the fastest as the best possible survival technique. We have long believed in bigger, better, more. I think that narrative has been so overused it has ceased to be effective, it has depleted the resources available around it, sucked all the air out of the room. There is room for another story, other skills to sit alongside it, a redistribution of some value back to other skills, other methods. There are other survival methods and skills in our evolution, in our makeup, things that have carried us this far and could carry us further still. If we let them.

11. The value of the highly sensitive

This chapter explores sensitivity from two angles: 1. What is good about being highly sensitive for the individual? 2. What is good about being highly sensitive for others? I want to know more about the positives, I want more language to understand this skill, this trait.

One of the big advantages of HSPs is their capacity for intense feeling. All of their feelings are intense, including the extremities – joy and sorrow. I can see how this might at first appear a negative, but just take a moment to reconsider. Joy is fundamental and visceral; it is in moments of joy that we often feel most alive. And the same can be said for sorrow in a slightly different way. Sorrow is painful, and all of us hope to avoid it. But, perversely, there are benefits to sadness and sorrow, including reducing judgemental bias, increased generosity and attention to external world detail. Sadness can help us become more authentic and connected.

The arts are a vehicle for us all to understand and see ourselves, individually and as a society. And in the arts, we often see and experience joy and sorrow, as a way of connecting with ourselves and with another's lived experience. The highly sensitive are exceptionally moved by arts and music – for example, I went to see a show called *Dressed*, created by This Egg and Made My Wardrobe, a show about female experience, sexual assault, the power to dress ourselves as an act of healing and friendship. There is a moment in the show where the woman, tired from sharing her experience of sexual assault, lies down under a pile of clothes, completely covered and silent. Her three friends wait and listen without saying anything, and though she is silent and not moving, they hold the space for her for a long time. After a while one of them picks up a microphone from a stand, walks across the stage and puts it down on the stage floor in front of the pile of clothes. Throughout the show I had been crying and laughing, stricken and overjoyed, but this one wordless action, offering space and voice to another out of love, destroyed me. Maybe because I had recently lost one of my lifelong dearest friends, not to death but because of the friendship ending due to misunderstanding, the pain of which was terrible. But it was more than that. These women had made, in a piece of art for people to see, a moment of such profound love that it physically hurt my heart – because it's something all of us need, we all need others, and they did it so beautifully, so simply, with such resonance. I almost couldn't take it. What they had made was so specific and so universal. It felt like a beautiful puncture wound. It felt like time and space folded in on itself and expanded back out.

I turned my face up to the ceiling of the theatre and stared at the stage lights and, as silently as possible, I cried and cried. For every person who has made space for another, for every person who has not. It got right inside my heart, and it still makes me cry with pain and happiness.

When I tell people about that experience, as evidence of the power of art, some laugh and look confused, some nod and nod and I can see all too well that they know that extremity of having been moved to a core emotional state by a piece of art. Often after an extraordinary experience at a gig or the theatre, I can't speak, which feels ironic being a writer – the only language I have at those moments is an emotional language of intense feeling. And I have realized that those moments often prove to be transformative in some way, sometimes facilitating moments of letting go, moving on, holding dear, being grateful.

I think this capacity to feel the extremities is an extraordinary gift. Sure, it is like living missing a layer of skin. But also, the feelings – isn't that what we are for? Isn't that the sound and touch of being alive? That is what I want – an alive life. Isn't that such a luxury, such a privilege, that if afforded should be relished? But we have a funny societal response to joy and sorrow. We present the idea that the ideal is to level through, to be moderate, to remain relatively unaffected by things. We congratulate people for remaining unaffected by things. I find that incomprehensible. Without the extremities, what have we got? We need joy and sorrow; we need intense emotion. Not all the time – how exhausting would that be? But some of the time, more than a little of the time. Wouldn't it be great if instead of saying, 'Well done for keeping a stiff upper lip' we said, 'Well done, you felt the feelings, that is being alive'?

Not only are those who are most sensitive capable of great feeling, but they are also naturally curious, exploring, absorbing, learning, thinking all the time. Curiosity makes our minds observant of new ideas and situations. It makes our minds active instead of passive. Massively challenging in a political and economic time that wishes us to keep our heads down and be compliant and unquestioning. Studies have shown that high levels of curiosity in adults lead to increased problem-solving and innovation. What a way to live, to always be interested, to keep wanting to know and notice.

Next, cognitive flexibility. Rigid thinking is what it says on the tin – I do things this way, this is what I believe and it will not change. Cognitive flexibility is the ability to adapt your behaviour to changing circumstances. It is the ability to switch between different concepts, to hold multiple ideas concurrently and shift our internal attention between them. As Lord Knight said in chapter 4, it's one of the key core skills for young people of the future, one that we all need to develop in such time of evolving change. Also, rational, logical thinking is the kind of thinking that computers can follow and be programmed to achieve. As technology takes over more and more of our professions that require obedience, uniformity, rationality, it places a premium on other types of thinking, such as cognitive flexibility. HSPs are constantly reading and processing extra information, and with that comes naturally the ability to hold multiple concepts concurrently. HSPs are great at understanding multiple realities, different points of view – they grasp nuance. Nuance, what a valuable and vanishing skill in a time of oppositional politics with no middle ground. It is a great resource to have a naturally flexible mind. A skill that will prove incredibly useful as we move forwards, the ability to imagine ourselves differently, to put down old ideas and examine new possibilities. A muscle we could all do with toning up. An ability that will be incredibly valuable when it is necessary to move forwards in a considered way into a dangerous future.

Really, that last one is about what HSPs offer to the people and communities around them. There is an aspect of this I feel a little conflicted about. There have been various things written on the function of HSPs as alarm systems – canaries in the coalmine.

To explain this image: miners would carry canaries in cages down into the mines. If dangerous gases such as carbon monoxide had gathered, the gases would kill the canary before they killed the miners, thus giving the miners a warning sign to exit. So a canary in a coalmine has come to signify something whose sensitivity is a useful early indicator of dangerous conditions. Basically, if the highly sensitive person finds the situation a problem, the rest of us might too.

Another extension of this metaphor is described by Dr Elaine Aron on her website, talking about when she met Janine Ramsey, a New Zealander working in the business sector, at an HSP conference. Janine showed Dr Aron her presentation on 'Roses in the Vineyard'. This explores the idea that in a vineyard, the grapes are susceptible to a lot of different diseases, year in, year out. And roses are sensitive to these same diseases. So roses are sometimes planted at the end of a row of vines and, because they are more susceptible, when disease inevitably comes along, the roses take the hit first and are early indicators to the grape-growers of a problem.

The reason I feel conflicted about this skill of HSPs is that it seems somewhat compromising to have one's value tied up in being a danger litmus: it indicates self-sacrifice for the good of the group. So it suggests that a lot of the value of HSPs is as sacrificial lambs. Nonetheless, it is a useful interpretation. I have long had this image of a group of deer grazing in a valley, interconnected family systems and kinships and rivalries all in tow within that group of deer – just grazing away, making sure they get the nutrients they need. Then some of those within the group sense something coming, something in the wind, a little earlier than others. It could be anything, a shadow, a rustle of grass, a smell. Those most likely to notice first are HSPs – that is what they do, they are always paying super-attention. So, let's say something dangerous does come, it's of use for them to communicate that information to the rest of the group. And that is another way in which they are canaries in the coalmine.

But what if we have developed a society that does not listen to the canaries, ignores infected rose bushes? What if the function of HSPs is to tell us what they notice, but we have made them largely redundant with the culture we are living in?

The job and benefit of HSPs are to tell us what they notice, because they are noticing more, reading deeper levels of sensory information, making connections – but we are not fully listening, and that undermines one of the skills that HSPs offer. And some of that is to do with it being incredibly inconvenient to call out a problem of the society we are living in now. We have this idea, which really shows how inflexible we are as a society, that nothing can change, that we must keep things as they are. Our governments and our politics currently lack the traits of detailed consideration and perception. We are in the midst of a mental health crisis, and a large proportion of the sufferers are HSPs, people more likely to notice if the birds change their behaviour, or the air starts to smell different, or if everyone around them is miserable about the living conditions and values of the society in which we exist. But are we listening to what that means for all of us?

HSPs often experience vivid dreams, sudden understandings, glimpses of information that are not explained. And I can see why this means HSPs often align with the culture of spirituality and find belonging and comfort there. As Dr Elaine Aron writes in *The Highly Sensitive Person*, there is something about HSPs as soulful and having great spirit – she terms them the priest class, with skills useful for nourishing society. She outlines several key roles and skills of the priest class, among them:

- Creating sacred space
- Prophesying
- Leading in the search for wholeness
- Writing the precepts of your religion
- Inspiring others in the search for meaning

I think these key roles and skills are useful indicators for understanding HSPs, and I am interested in how we can anchor some of those in the everyday.

Creating sacred space
Some people can make the everyday sacred, the spaces they inhabit and create for others – through empathy, care, aesthetics. HSPs often have an extraordinary ability to understand the synthesis of a space – what conditions are needed to make the space more comfortable with itself; for example, turning overhead fluorescent lights off and turning a lamp on. Moving a desk that is facing the wrong way. Adjusting curtains.

I think with the right kind of attention all space has the potential to be comfortable with itself and HSPs are often the ideal people to make these changes. I think this type of synthesis can feel sacred.

I think often of Kettle's Yard in Cambridge, a place created by Jim and Helen Ede, a house that is also an art gallery, where visitors are allowed to sit on chairs, interact with the space and the art present. My experience of attending Kettle's Yard is one of almost painful realization – that here a careful space has been made to hold people; the feeling of that is so palpable that it is humbling, and in that humbling it feels sacred. Care is sacred in many ways. I think HSPs often have the potential to create those spaces, spaces to hold the mess and honesty and many stories of what it means to be a person, and it feels so very generous and different from the everyday.

Creating sacred space can also mean more than a literal space. We each create a space each time we connect with another person. HSPs, with their gift for understanding the multiples of human experience and opinion, are very well placed to create spaces for people to come together who do not have shared views. We are currently living in a time of oppositional, divisive cultures that filter down and through – we have political parties whose language is based around defence and attack, an online trend of cancel culture, a relationship culture of ghosting people. We eliminate difficulty, and I understand the impulse to do so, but I also wonder if HSPs have something to offer out of our skillset – the nuance and complexity of thought to let difference sit side by side. The world is changing rapidly, we are entering uncertain times. Spaces such as those that allow for a coming together are rare and sacred.

Prophesying

It is understood that there are those among us who have a gift for being able to predict what is coming over the hill, towards us on the wind, which way interpersonal dynamics might shift, what the next occurrence might be in a sequence of happenings. This is often understood as a sort of psychic shamanism – and although I am not against that, I cannot rest the weight of my instinct on it. It does not feel like a complete explanation to me. I do accept that there are those of us who have, for example, a vivid dream, that tells us through imagery the way that something might go. I think it is a capacity to be continuously reading extra levels of information from people and environment, a sort of constant knitting of information, on a conscious and unconscious level, and due to this there emerges an ability to anticipate what is going to happen next. In short, it's paying attention in a profound way.

Leading in the search for wholeness

This one makes me a little nervous. It feels a little grandiose to propose leading others in the search for wholeness. Surely, we all lead ourselves. But I do think that HSPs are more likely than others, through a process of not fitting in, to know themselves very well, to be authentic. And in addition, being internal-processing thought dwellers and being motivated by meaning, to have quite a fully formed sense of what wholeness means to them. I interpret wholeness as an understanding of what gives you and your life meaning, and a connection to it. That definition is bound to be different from person to person. But HSPs are more likely to be drawn to jobs that involve wholeness in some way – or at least the instinct for wholeness, such as teaching, nursing, psychological support, heritage or the arts. I do think that HSPs are more likely to question their place in things, and what their actions in the world contribute to.

So the values of HSPs are many. Quite a list, including but not exclusively: extremities of emotion such as joy and sorrow; creativity, curiosity, cognitive flexibility, nuanced understanding; meaning-driven, intuitive empathy; noticing of warning signs and opportunity; connecting information; the ability to offer detailed consideration; seeing the big picture. And I think the ultimate value lives in a phrase Barbara Allen used back in chapter 5: 'So we don't explode everything.'

Conclusion: An era of sensitivity?

We live in capitalism. Its power seems inescapable.
So did the divine right of kings. Any human power
can be resisted and changed by human beings.
URSULA K LE GUIN

I wrote this book because I felt and still feel it is absolutely
necessary for sensitivity to have a more developed, rounded
story, and I wanted to help try to dig that out. I wanted a short,
sharp list containing positive understandings of sensitivity,
drawn from extensive research undertaken by others and from
conversations with interviewees in this book:

- Sensitivity means paying extra attention to people and
  environment
- It is a basic common trait – neither good nor bad
- Sensitivity primes us to make an appropriate response to
  person or environment – appropriate response is so that 'we
  don't explode things'
- HSPs are likely to have high emotional intelligence, be
  authentic, curious throughout their lives, conscientious,

motivated by meaning, highly empathic
- HSPs are possibly highly intuitive
- HSPs are likely to notice things others may not
- Sensitivity is social glue, it is the reason we are able to live in groups and sustain that
- HSPs are usually the first to notice and be affected by less than ideal conditions, threats and potential opportunities
- HSPs and sensitivity offer us cognitive flexibility, detail-noticing, perceptive, big-picture thinking, pattern-noticing
- HSPs are likely to be story-holders, space-makers, ritual creators, understanding the importance of nuance
- The skill of sensitivity facilitates cooperation, distributed leadership, the connection with environment and nature outside of ourselves
- Sensitivity is a trait and a skill
- Sensitivity and its component parts have been good strategy in our evolutionary past
- It is an old part of us, which might be of use in the future.

I find it helpful to have things as a list. This list forms and affirms the building blocks of a better story for sensitivity. I read that list and feel myself shift, come apart and reform in a new shape. That list filters through the story I have about myself, makes me soften, lower my defences. It makes me feel I can face the world in a bolder way, with articulation and evidence, that sensitivity is something of value. It makes me feel I have more explanation to offer others about their sensitivity. It makes me feel I have artillery, if I need it. Because yes, there is this huge proportion of the population who are HSPs. And yes, this trait is in all of us in various degrees. But there are still many, many people out there who hold a fundamental belief that sensitivity is weak, lacking value, something that needs to be educated out. It is hard to find an answer for 'Well, what is sensitivity for?' in the face of such solid, entrenched conviction. I hope this list offers some language – artillery, if needed – to help rebalance some belief systems. I do not buy into the idea that there are some people whose beliefs systems remain the same no matter what. We are all permeable. Change acts on us all, eventually. And even if there are those who cannot be persuaded, understanding our difference is still of immense value. It shows us what we are, what we are not and what we could each be.

I realize, coming to the close of this book, how very much my motivation to undertake this process, to have this conversation with you, was shaped around need and love. I wanted to better understand myself, to change my story so that I could help my daughter positively shape who she is. I wanted to better understand you and, if you need it, to help you better round out your story. I have realized how vital, how alive, our self-stories are. How very much humans thrive on internal narrative, how it shapes how and what we do, who we connect with and how. Prior to this process, I had dramatically underestimated the power of these stories, how they run right through us, like messages in sticks of rock. How there is great power in taking control of that story, understanding who and what we are, what we offer, where we are challenged.

I think of all the stories I read my daughter, I think of what she learns from me, the things she sees and hears in the world. What story is forming inside her? What is her messaging? Have I done enough? How will I know? And even as I write that, I know too that the ultimate act of parenting is the slow release of our children into their own choices. Trusting that those stories inside them will keep them afloat, like boats that we can only hope carry them where they want to go. To a destination that understands them to be of value.

I think back to that moment of watching my daughter circle the playgroup, me willing her to just be like the others. I feel very differently about that now. Yes, it looks like she is not participating, and it is very easy to read that as a problem. And yes, I strongly feel the social pressure to get her to conform. But no. No. She is operating in the way suitable for who she is. And who she is is as important as any other. She is circling the room mapping layers of information, she is listening to the air and the form of the room, the moods that move between people, she is noticing body language, the task ask, she can hear the weather on the roof of the hall, she is taking in information, processing before she decides or acts. Following the wisdom of my mum, I am going to help her find her way in the world by 'stroking feathers that have been pushed in all the wrong directions'.

My daughter will most likely grow in different ways; she has different skills. She is one of life's noticers and intense feelers. She will live her life, I imagine, deeply. And yes, quite possibly she will live like she is missing a layer of skin, connecting with others' feelings and needs. And I am not going to lie: it is, even at this point, incredibly tempting, by way of protecting my child, to teach her to pad up, to toughen up, to desensitize. But no. Instead I am going to teach her tactics, strategies to manage her own feelings, the loudness of her own voice in the world. We each need to learn to bear ourselves, we are feeling beings, no matter the degree.

When I began this book, I thought it was a story solely about individuals learning to tolerate who they are, through changing an internal narrative. And it is. But to my great surprise it is also about something else. It is a story about resource and the future.

We are living in a time of realization, realization of old stories that are no longer useful to us. And one of those old stories is the story that says sensitivity is weak. Sensitivity is not for anything. Sensitivity is a problem.

But that is not true. It is an old story that needs taking out of the filing cabinet and burning. It's an old story that needs digging out of us. Sensitivity is not weak. It is not a problem. And it is for a great many things. I don't really get on board with the whole 'one group is better than the other', but allow me a moment. It takes massive strength to live without a layer of skin. It takes huge resourcefulness to navigate a system not designed in your image. The real story of sensitivity is one of profound vulnerability and resilience, care, empathy. The real story of sensitivity is much more everyday, much more mythic than we think. Sensitivity is fundamental to who we are, and I think it might be fundamental to where we go next.

We have lived many societies and cultures, and many of them have not survived. I think about the shelf in my kitchen, of bits of pots, bone and flint. Fragments of us found in fields. We are so vulnerable, and yet we seem so solid. That solidity, that invulnerability, is a lie. We are the threads between us, the careful ecosystem of us and the sky. We are ourselves and those we love. We are our own achievements and our collaboration. And we are living on the edge, at a pivotal moment; what we do next, and how, is more vital than it has ever been. It is incredibly tempting to bury ourselves in the myth of our permanence, to carry on with the values of bigger, better, more, and the toughest succeed. But there are those before us who have made this mistake. There are bits of them everywhere in fields.

Good old sensitivity, like an unassuming dog, lurking around in the background. Might it be a good moment to consider what else we have available to us that might be useful in figuring out what happens next and how? Because there really is need to consider what happens next. I think back to the man who told me that understanding his sensitivity had given him back the sun, I think of how long he spent in the dark. I think of how lightly we litter the phrase 'I guess you're just a little too sensitive' and how it hits like a stone. I think of our culture of hyper-productivity. I think of who we include in decision-making processes. What leadership we vote in. I think of Wendy Showell Nicholas telling me that if a workplace culture is wrong, HSPs will most likely be affected first. And that means the culture is wrong for everyone. I think of our icebergs collapsing, forest fires spreading. We are badly in need of appropriate response. The world around us is telling us a story; it is saying, there is a cost to this set of values. What we do next in response to that message is crucial. I think of my grandfather, Da, his fingers moving back and forth, back and forth on the arms of the green velvet armchair, 'What happens next...what happens next?'

We have two choices, really, in how to fill that story gap. Carry on as normal with the story of bigger, better, more commodified individualism, competition, accumulation. Do we feel confident that story is going to lead us in the right direction? I don't. Do we have another alternative? Yes. We have an older story, a story of collaboration, cooperation, empathy, noticing, considered appropriate response. It is easy to feel pessimistic about what we face. But look at us, look at the variety we contain. What potential! We are so beautifully adaptable. So very capable of resilience and change. We are standing on the shoulders of the skills that live within us. Competition is just one of our many abilities. We are more than we think we are, we are more than the structures we live within, we are more than the story our culture tells. And just one of the things we have available is our great and innate capacity for sensitivity.

The following quote is attributed to the anthropologist Dr Margaret Mead. She was asked by a student what she considered to be the earliest sign of civilization in a culture. The student expected Dr Mead to talk about fishhooks or clay pots or grinding stones. But no. She said that the first sign of civilization in an ancient culture was a femur (thighbone) that had been broken and then healed. She explained that in the animal kingdom if you break your leg, you die. You cannot run from danger, get to the river for a drink or hunt for food. No animal survives a broken leg bone long enough for the bone to heal.

> A broken femur that has healed is evidence that
> someone has taken the time to stay with the one that
> fell, has bound up the wound, has carried the person
> to safety and has tended the person through recovery.
> Helping someone else through difficulty is where
> civilization starts.

Mead also said, 'Never believe that a few caring people can't change the world. For, indeed, that's all who ever have.'

Yes, I can hear the loud and domineering voice of capitalism that says, 'This is all we are.' But I refuse that. We are more. We are a civilization founded on the connections between us. Because we stopped to notice, because we waited and cared long enough for bones to heal.

Civilization is this struggle between short-term self-interest and long-term strategy. We are competition and cooperation. Cruelty and empathy. And if we are smart about it, if we consider what is an appropriate response, it's not hard to see that cooperation is the best possible strategy, because what needs to be achieved cannot be achieved solo. And what skill aids cooperation? Yes – sensitivity! Professor Martin Nowak and Roger Highfield wrote a book called *Super Cooperators* that caused quite a stir. Within it they say: 'Cooperation can draw living matter upward to higher levels of organization...today we face a stark choice: we can either move up to the next stage of evolutionary complexity, or we can go into decline, even become extinct.'

And I can hear as I write this, the internalized voice that says nothing can change, how we do things is unchangeable. And to that voice I offer Rebecca Solnit from her book *Hope in the Dark*:

> ...the mingled complacency and despair that says
> things cannot change, will not change, and we do
> not have power to change them. You'd have to be
> an amnesiac or at least ignorant of history and even
> current events to fail to see that our country and our
> world have always been changing, are in the midst
> of great and terrible changes, and are occasionally
> changed through the power of the popular will and
> idealistic movement. Climate now demands we
> summon up the force to leave behind the Age of
> Fossil Fuel (and maybe with it some of the Age of
> Capitalism).

We are at a road split, with the advantage of a brief vantage point. Look one way and you will see the legacy, inheritance and innovation of industrialism. Look the other and you will see, well, not much – an unknown future penned in by threat. And the only thing we know is that we have to find a way on. I think of us standing on our doorsteps on a Thursday evening during the COVID-19 pandemic, clapping and clapping and clapping for nurses, doctors, carers – those out there fighting COVID on our behalf. I think of that excruciating moment of fragility and disruption to our lives, to capitalism and industry. Has it caused us to pause and reflect, to think about what's next? That moment of fragility showed us how we are vulnerable, all of us.

There is opportunity inside rupture. Opportunity to consider doing things differently. For example, during the pandemic, there was great talk, nay promise, of pay remuneration for those working in care-based professions, teachers, nurses and others. But that did not materialize. We had a momentary glimpse of the profoundly human value of sensitivity. And it is that, I hope, we will hold on to. We are so permeable. We are so affected by each other. And we have this great skill, written into us, all of us, to different degrees. This great ability to know and understand what one another need and feel. To provide care. To be part of our environment. To notice, plan, cooperate. And that great ability is not in us by accident, it is there for our survival, of the individual and the group. We are such storymakers. We can make the next bit of the story.

Just in case you remain unconvinced, because I realize language plays such a powerful role in who we carry with us, allow me to phrase it in more economic terms. Sensitivity equates to appropriate reaction. And appropriate reaction means a response appropriate to the occasion. Our house is on fire. So, what is an appropriate reaction? Option 1: Use the values of the system we currently exist in, the values of capitalism, to try to find a way forwards. Option 2: try a new way or, rather, an old way. Care, notice, feel, consider, intuit, cooperate between skillsets – offer an appropriate response. When empathy collides with a belief system, it provokes action.

In that circular way things often go, I am going to close this book with something from the start. Words my mum sent me and my siblings out the door with each morning: 'Be kind, be sensitive, look out for other people.'

***

Thank you for spending time in this book. By means of farewell, I wanted to offer you a poem, like chocolate with coffee at the end of a meal. In 2019 I was commissioned by Forest Fringe (an extraordinary theatre organization, a community of artists who make space for experimentation and risk) to write a poem for a piece called *Museum of Hope Against the Dark* for Latitude Festival, inspired by Rebecca Solnit's book *Hope Against the Dark*. Installed deep in the forest at a festival hung a lightbulb erratically flashing, seemingly broken – in fact, transmitting in Morse code a poem containing a message of hope. The audience were given Morse code to help them translate. This is that poem.

> Hi,
> I was wondering when you would want to talk,
> I am so glad you made it past the barrier,
> I hope you are comfy, and please,
> don't be afraid
> you have just got your eyes closed.
>
> If I leave long gaps, it's because
> sometimes there are bits of light
> that open you right up
> and then the trees lean in
> and the air listens.

But to keep the conversation going I will tell you
when I was 14, my friend Medina
sat me down on the top step of the tech building
and said *If you feel hopeless, think of a T Rex
wrestling a duvet cover onto a duvet.*

But I want to talk about roads,
and how it looks like we have run out,
how we have been driving a while now,
in fact, for ages, down all roads we were told to go,
and we have seen ourselves past so many cities and
    barbed wire and field mist,
and now we've reached a big yellow barrier,
and no one is coming to show us the way.

So, we will need to go cross-country from here, OK,
    love –
your feet will harden so it will be fine
and you know as much as you are ever going to need
and if you look between the trees,
you will see others climbing gate posts,
vaulting fences like rodeo riders,
saying goodbye to the broken machine.

Here, let's build a fire, feed it policy papers,
from what a distance the flames will be seen,
even through closed eyelids the warmth will seep.

Your eyes are open.
You are so comfy.
I am so glad you made it past the barrier.

Notes

PART 1

Introduction

3. *That same day I got an email from* BBC Radio 4 programme *Sensitive Souls* for *Four Thought*, produced by Giles Edwards, https://www.bbc.co.uk/programmes/b0832rjl

3. *HSP – Dr Elaine Aron* Aron, E N, 1999. *The Highly Sensitive Person: How to Thrive When the World Overwhelms You*, London: Thorsons

Chapter 1: Self-worth

13. *Robin Skeates* Skeates, R, 2011. 'Making Sense of World Art: An Archaeological Perspective', *World Art* 1(1), 143–9, https://doi.org/10.1080/21500894.2011.534595

Chapter 2: Highly Sensitive

32. *Highly Sensitive test* https://hsperson.com/test/highly-sensitive-test/

38. *Rebecca Solnit* Solnit, R, 2018. *Call Them by Their True Names: American Crises (and Essays)*, London: Granta

38. *The age of narcissism* Karasu, T B, 2011. *Gotham Chronicles: The Culture of Sociopathy*, Lanham, MD: Rowman & Littlefield

Chapter 3: Somewhere on the scale

47. *Documentary-making with Giles* BBC Radio 4 documentary, https://www.bbc.co.uk/programmes/m0007bkj

49. *Quality of the parenting they receive* Lionetti, F, Aron, E N, Aron, A, Klein, D N, & Pluess, M, 2019. 'Observer-rated Environmental Sensitivity Moderates Children's Response to Parenting Quality in Early Childhood', *Developmental Psychology* 55(11), 2389–402, https://doi.org/10.1037/dev0000795

Chapter 4: We are what we teach

61. *I have an interest in education*   TED talk by Sir Ken Robinson, 2006. 'Do Schools Kill Creativity?', https://www.ted.com/talks/sir_ken_robinson_do_schools_kill_creativity/transcript?language=en

62. *In August 2021 the* Guardian article by Richard Beard, 'Why Public Schoolboys Like Me and Boris Johnson Aren't Fit to Run Our Country', https://www.theguardian.com/education/2021/aug/08/public-schoolboys-boris-johnson-sad-little-boys-richard-beard

62. *The article went on to quote* Schaverien, J, 2015. *Boarding School Syndrome: The Psychological Trauma of the 'Privileged' Child*, London: Routledge

70. *English Pastoral* Rebanks, J, 2020. *English Pastoral: An Inheritance*, London: Penguin Books

85. *An article on Teachstone* Mamie Morrow, 'Teacher Sensitivity: A Sensitive Coaching Topic', http://info.teachstone.com/blog/teacher-sensitivity-a-sensitive-coaching-topic

92. *American philosopher Martha C Nussbaum* Nussbaum, M C, 2012. *Not for Profit: Why Democracy Needs the Humanities*, Princeton, NJ: Princeton University Press

92. *David Bridges* Bridges, D & Schendan, H E, 2019. 'Sensitive Individuals Are More Creative', *Personality and Individual Differences*, 142, 186–95, https://doi.org/10.1016/j.paid.2018.09.015

93. *In 1968 George Land, with Beth Jarman* Land, G, and Jarman, B, https://www.ideatovalue.com/crea/nickskillicorn/2016/08/evidence-children-become-less-creative-time-fix/

95. *Each educational system* Scarleth Bulga Paez, 'Each Educational System Is a Mirror that Reflects the Culture of the Society', https://www.scribd.com/document/163413099/Each-Educational-System-is-a-Mirror-That-Reflects-the-Culture-of-the-Society

Chapter 5: Sensitive challenges

103. *Barbara Allen* founder and director of the National Centre for High Sensitivity (2010–19), www.growingunlimited.co.uk

115. *Psych Collective with Dr Al Griskaitis* The Psych Collective, https://www.thepsychcollective.com/

PART 2

Chapter 6: Sensitivity and the past

140. *Professor Roger Walsh* Walsh, R, 1994. 'The Making of a Shaman: Calling, Training, and Culmination', *The Journal of Humanistic Psychology*, 34(3), 7–30, https://doi.org/10.1177/00221678940343003

141. *Professor Ingold's paper* Ingold, T, 2013. 'Dreaming of Dragons: On the Imagination of Real Life', *The Journal of the Royal Anthropological Institute*, 19(4), 734–52, https://doi.org/10.1111/1467-9655.12062

143. *He directed me to a paper due* Ingold, T, 2021. 'Chapter 18. The World in a Basket', in *Imagining for Real. Essays on Creation, Attention and Correspondence,* 273–84, London: Routledge. The quote on page 145 ('I believe this can be done') refers to Tello-Ramos, M C, Hurly, T A, Barclay, M, and Healy, S D, 'Hummingbirds Modify Their Routes to Avoid a Poor Location', *Learning & Behavior* (2021), https://doi.org/10.3758/s13420-021-00476-3

Chapter 8: Gut instinct

178. *Professor Joel Pearson* Lufityanto, G, Donkin, C, & Pearson, J, 2016. 'Measuring Intuition: Nonconscious Emotional Information Boosts Decision Accuracy and Confidence', *Psychological Science*, 27(5), 622–34, https://doi.org/10.1177/0956797616629403

179. *Amanda Hooten* 'Sixth Sense: The Science Behind Intuition', Amanda Hooten for *Sydney Morning Herald*, https://www.smh.com.au/lifestyle/life-and-relationships/sixth-sense-the-science-behind-intuition-20210304-p577wm.html

181. *The article in the* Observer Robson, D, 2019. *The Intelligence Trap: Why Smart People Make Stupid Mistakes – and How to Make Wiser Decisions,* London: Hodder & Stoughton

Chapter 9: Working it

186 *As Eilis Lawlor* Lawlor, E, Kersley, H, and Steed, S, joint article for the New Economics Foundation, https://neweconomics.org/2009/12/a-bit-rich

193. *Desert Island Discs* BBC Radio 4, Nazir Afzal, https://www.bbc.co.uk/programmes/m000ydp1

Chapter 10: Why is it in us?

220. *Ellen Dissanayake* Dissanayake, E, 1988. *What Is Art For?*, Seattle, WA: University of Washington Press

220. *Denis Dutton* Dutton, D, 2010. *The Art Instinct: Beauty, Pleasure, and Human Evolution*, Oxford: Oxford University Press

221. *Mothers and Others* Hrdy, S B, 2009. *Mothers and Others: The Evolutionary Origins of Mutual Understanding*, Cambridge, MA: Belknap Press, Harvard University Press

222. *Marilyn Strathern* Strathern, M, 1988. *The Gender of the Gift: Problems with Women and Problems with Society in Melanesia*, London: University of California Press

Conclusion: An Era of Sensitivity

259. *We live in capitalism* Ursula K Le Guin speech at National Book Awards, https://youtu.be/Et9Nf-rsALk

265. *A broken femur* quote attributed to Margaret Mead in an article in Forbes, https://www.forbes.com/sites/remyblumenfeld/2020/03/21/how-a-15000-year-old-human-bone-could-help-you-through-the--coronavirus/?sh=2b345d837e9b

265. *Never believe that* Mead, M, 2005. *The World Ahead: An Anthropologist Anticipates the Future, The Study of Contemporary Western Culture*, 6, Oxford: Berghahn

266. *Professor Martin Nowak* Nowak, M A with Highfield, R, 2011. *Super Cooperators: Altruism, Evolution, and Why We Need Each Other to Succeed*, Edinburgh: Canongate

266. *And to that voice I offer* Solnit, R, 2016. *Hope in the Dark: Untold Histories, Wild Possibilities,* Edinburgh: Canongate

268. *Forest Fringe* Hannah Jane Walker

Acknowledgements

In typical style, in order to thank people, I need to tell you a story. In 2016, I made a radio piece about sensitivity for BBC Radio 4 with brilliant producer Giles Edwards, and hundreds of strangers got in touch with me. If it hadn't been for those strangers, I wouldn't have had the confidence to ask the BBC to do a second piece. Thank you for reaching out. It's a powerful thing to do. The BBC commissioned a documentary exploring the subject further, and Giles Edwards once again made that process a dream.

I sometimes make theatre and decided it would be a good theatre show. The National Centre for Writing, Chris Gribble, Peggy Hughes, Alison McFarlane and others supported me in this with their time and residency space. At Cambridge Junction, Matt Burman and Ema Boswood gave me feedback, structure and encouragement. Arts Council England funded the work. I made the show, premiered it at Norfolk and Norwich Festival at Norwich Arts Centre, programmed by Pasco Kelvin, then toured it on to Colchester Arts Centre, programmed by Antony Roberts; Cambridge Junction, programmed by Matt Burman; and Roundhouse London, programmed by Malú Ansaldo. At each of those venues is a programmer or venue director – absolute gems, people who put in real graft and love to keep the cultural heart of the UK beating. The show was also shaped in its early stages by Kirsty Housley, Katie Bonna and Shon Dale

Jones, and supported and shaped over the course of the run by Francesca Beard.

During the run of the show at the Roundhouse, I got an email from a lady called Kate Adams, who worked for a publisher, Octopus, inviting me for a cup of tea. She had come to see the show and wanted to chat. We met and she said, 'Would you write this as a book?'

I laughed. 'I can't write a book! I can't even write to the end of the line. I have written poetry for so long, I hit return automatically after seven words.'

'Well, think about it. If you reconsider, send me an email,' Kate said.

Time carried on, life went on, and I made other work in other art forms. And then the pandemic hit. At that point 100 per cent of my work involved being with a live audience or group of participants for a workshop. Within two days I had lost all future income and work and, like all parents, was suddenly juggling full-time childcare. No furlough if you are freelance. And if you are a working mother, the government freelance support scheme penalizes you for lower income periods while your child was preschool. I have stood on the brink of ruin before, and thought what are the arts for, why did I choose this? And knowing that, I regularly have online sessions with artist wellbeing practitioner Louise Platt, an extraordinary person who really understands how to help artists navigate...being artists. In conversation with Lou Platt, she fed back to me that I kept saying, 'I just want to write.' Once I actually heard what she was saying, I remembered the seed of an idea planted by Kate Adams at Octopus. I got back in touch, said, 'OK, what do I need to do?' and she generously supported me through the proposal-writing process.

I soon realized I needed an agent, that I didn't really know what I was doing. And so, I called on a few people I know who are authors and have gone through this process themselves. Author Joe Dunthorne, who explained to me what an agent does and why. Tom Chivers, author and director of Penned in the Margins, who talked to me about his process with his book *London Clay* and recommended his agent very highly. Dan Richards, author, told me what to look out for. I also called author and old flatmate Joe Minihane and poet Luke Wright, who gave me, as ever, confidence. I am very grateful to these people who at this point gave me their time, shared their experience. It is a real kindness and one I won't forget. Most of these writers I met as the result of studying together at the University of East Anglia. As the result of this advice-giving, I began working with agent Sophie Scard at United Agents. And because of all I mention above, the book was commissioned. I rented an office space I love from Henry Rowe in the small town I live in – my first working space outside of the home in fifteen years. And I started the process of writing this book.

It has been a lifeboat during a time where professional survival was unlikely. And when I began, that is all I thought of. During the process, however, I have come to realize that it was a lifeboat of many kinds, that I have always wanted to write and explore in this way, that I love writing. So above all, I am grateful to Kate Adams for taking the time to come and see the show, for planting the idea. You have given me something I didn't know I needed, and I am very grateful.

In each chapter of the book is an interview with a specialist. The route to those specialists has been led sometimes by strangers I emailed out the blue, but often through people I knew already. Thank you, Nicola Buckley, Head of Public Engagement at Cambridge University; Fiona L Bennett and Chris Higgins,

The Map Consortium; Charles Gladstone, The Good Life Experience; Dr Jo Vergunst; Laura Turvill.

To each contributor in this book: it was such a delight to spend time talking with you. You were so generous with your time, explanations, insights and humanity, and I am in awe of you all: Dr Bianca Acevedo, Kate Northam-Walker, Wendy Nicholas, Gemma, Professor David Deming, Christine Garner, Professor Michael Pluess, Dr Elaine Aron, Dr David Chicoine, Dr Simone Schnall, Jessica O'Garr, Dr Nick Spencer, Dr Nikhil Chaudhary, Chris Thompson, Barbara Allen, the Rt Hon Lord Jim Knight.

None of our accomplishments are ours alone. To the following people, thank you for sustaining, inspiring and tolerating me: my closest friends: Rachel Walker, Dr Emma Short, Emma Spearing, Jenny Holland, David Potter, Rachel Mariner. In particular, thank you to Dr Emma Short, who patiently proofread this manuscript before I submitted it to the publishers and told me I could do it. Louise Platt, artist wellbeing practitioner, who has been an invaluable source of inspiration and support, leading me to this book. Sophie Scard, my agent at United Agents, who has taught me so much so fast. Natalie Bradley, senior editor at Octopus Books, who has been so welcoming, articulate and kind. Thank you to Octopus Books for taking a chance on the book. And to all of the staff at Octopus who make all the magic happen behind the scenes, you do it very smoothly.

Though book acknowledgements are meant to be credits for the book, there are some people who have supported my development as an artist, to whom I would like to say a really heartfelt thank you. There are those who close doors, and those who open them – and you have opened doors for me into the arts: Jacqui Smith, Jonathan Holloway, Matt Burman, Chris Gribble, Francesca Beard, Chris Thorpe, Luke Wright, Lora Stimpson.

ACKNOWLEDGEMENTS

Thank you, Jonathan Holloway, for reading and annotating this manuscript with funny comments in the margins before I submitted it. Thank you, Matt Burman, for picking me up when I fall down and helping me see new ways on. Thank you, Francesca Beard, for sharing with me the strength of a woman who takes stage space. Thank you, Chris Gribble, for making space, for telling me the truth.

At heart I am a poet, and there are two poets who I began writing with, who I write with weekly and to whom I am grateful for getting me through lockdown, for holding me equal: John Osborne and Joe Dunthorne.

To those who have cared for our child, at school, nursery, childminders – Jess Dickinson, Colette Loveday, Fran Beale, thank you for keeping her happy, nourished and loved.

To my family, the Walkers, Brien, Kate, Rachel, Alice, Charlie, you big messy gang of sensitives – home is sometimes the very best inspiration. To my parents-in-law, Rhona and Jeremy – thank you for always being kind and helping out. To my grandparents, Professor John and Rachel Northam, Joan and George Jarman, Pauline and Brien Walker. Grandma Joan says we should each 'hitch our wagon to a star'.

In particular, thank you to my dad, Brien – for nagging and nagging and nagging me to write a book. I was listening. And thank you for taking me to the local library on Saturdays.

And to my mum, Kate, thank you for teaching me how to feel and know and care, thanks for untangling my hair, staying at parties with me and for never telling me my sensitivity was a problem.

To my husband, Dr Oscar Aldred, for loving me all the way through, for troubleshooting, inspiring and motivating me. For holding our lives steady while I wrote this.

To my gift daughter, Unnur Aldred, thank you for finding and translating the poem at the start of this book. For always bringing such joy home.

To my daughter, Thea, thank you for the inspiration and all the love.

Index